THE BOMBAY CITY POLICE

THE BOMBAY CITY POLICE:

A HISTORICAL SKETCH,

1672-1916

S. M. EDWARDES

GYAN

Published by

GYAN

Gyan Publishing House
5, Ansari Road
Daryaganj, New Delhi-110002
Phone: 011-47034999, 9811692060
E-mail: books@gyanbooks.com

Distribution Network
gyanbooks.com
India, USA, Canada, UK, Australia

ISBN: 978-93-6920-237-9 (HB)

First Published, 1923

2nd Impression 2025

Printed at: Gyan Press, Delhi.

THE BOMBAY CITY POLICE
Author: S. M. EDWARDES

THE BOMBAY CITY POLICE

THE BOMBAY CITY POLICE

A HISTORICAL SKETCH

1672-1916

BY

S. M. EDWARDES, C.S.I., C.V.O.,

formerly of the Indian Civil Service and sometime Commissioner of Police, Bombay

HUMPHREY MILFORD
OXFORD UNIVERSITY PRESS
LONDON BOMBAY CALCUTTA MADRAS
1923

PREFACE

I have been prompted to prepare this brief record of the past history and growth of the Bombay Police Force by the knowledge that, except for a few paragraphs in Volume II of the *Gazetteer of Bombay City and Island*, no connected account exists of the police administration of the City. Considering how closely interwoven with the daily life of the mass of the population the work of the Force has always been, and how large a contribution to the welfare and progress of the City has been made by successive Commissioners of Police, it seems well to place permanently on record in an accessible form the more important facts connected with the early arrangements for watch and ward and crime-prevention, and to describe the manner in which the Heads of the Force carried out the heavy responsibilities assigned to them.

The year 1916 is a convenient date for the conclusion of this historical sketch ; for in September of that year commenced the violent agitation for Home Rule which under varying names and varying leadership, and despite concessions and political reforms, kept India in a state of unrest during the following five or six years.

Other considerations also suggest that the narrative may close most fitly in the year preceding the memorable pronouncement in Parliament, which ushered in the recent constitutional reforms. No one can foretell what changes may hereafter take place in the character and constitution of the City Police Force; but it is improbable that the Force can remain unaffected by the altered character of the general administration. Ere old conditions and old landmarks disappear, it seems to me worth while to compile a succinct history of the Force, as it existed before the era of "democratic" reform.

PREFACE

I am indebted to the present Acting Commissioner of Police for the photographs of the portraits hanging in the Head Police Office and of the types of constabulary; to the Record-Keeper at the India Office for giving me access to various police reports and official papers dating from 1859 to 1916; and to Mr. Sivaram K. Joshi, 1st clerk in the Commissioner's office, who spent much of his leisure time in making inquiries and framing answers to various queries which the Bombay Government kindly forwarded at my request to the Head Police Office.

S. M. EDWARDES

London, 1923

CONTENTS

ILLUSTRATIONS

THE BOMBAY CITY POLICE
A HISTORICAL SKETCH
1672–1916

CHAPTER I

THE BHANDARI MILITIA
1672–1800

A perusal of the official records of the early period of British rule in Bombay indicates that the credit of first establishing a force for the prevention of crime and the protection of the inhabitants belongs to Gerald Aungier, who was appointed Governor of the Island in 1669 and filled that office with conspicuous ability until his death at Surat in 1677. Amidst the heavy duties which devolved upon him as President of Surat and Governor of the Company's recently acquired Island,[1] and at a time when the Dutch, the Portuguese, the Mogul, the Sidi and the Marathas offered jointly and severally a serious menace to the Company's trade and possessions, Aungier found leisure to organize a rude militia under the command of *Subehdars,* who were posted at Mahim, Sewri, Sion and other chief points of the Island.[2] This force was intended primarily for military protection, as a supplement to the regular garrison. That it was also employed on duties which would now be performed by the civil police, is clear from a letter of December 15, 1673, from Aungier and his council to the Court of Directors, in which the chief features of the Island and its administrative arrangements are described in considerable

1. Charles II transferred Bombay to the E. I. Company in 1668.
2. Gazetteer of Bombay City and Island, Vol. II, 238.

detail.[1] After mentioning the strength of the forces at Bombay and their distribution afloat and ashore, the letter proceeds:—

> "There are also three companies of militia, one at Bombay, one at Mahim, and one at Mazagon, consisting of Portuguese black Christians. More confidence can be placed in the Moors, Bandareens and Gentus than in them, because the latter are more courageous and show affection and goodwill to the English Government. These companies are exercised once a month at least, and serve as *night-watches against surprise and robbery.*"

A little while prior to Aungier's death, when John Petit was serving under him as Deputy Governor of Bombay, this militia numbered from 500 to 600, all of whom were landholders of Bombay. Service in the militia was in fact compulsory on all owners of land, except "the Braminys (Brahmans) and Bannians (Banias)," who were allowed exemption on a money payment.[2] The majority of the rank and file were Portuguese Eurasians ("black Christians"), the remainder including Muhammadans ("Moors"), who probably belonged chiefly to Mahim, and Hindus of various castes, such as "Sinays" (Shenvis), "Corumbeens" (Kunbis) and "Coolys" (Kolis).[3] The most important section of the Hindu element in this force of military night-watchmen was that of the Bhandaris ("Bandareens"), whose ancestors formed a settlement in Bombay in early ages, and whose modern descendants still cherish traditions of the former military and political power of their caste in the north Konkan.

The militia appears to have been maintained more or less at full strength during the troubled period of Sir John Child's governorship (1681-90). It narrowly escaped

1. Gazetteer of Bombay City and Island, Vol. II, pp. 65 ff.
2. R. and O. Strachey, *Keigwin's Rebellion*, p. 19 and App. E.
3. The letter of December 15, 1673, from Aungier and Council mentions these as some of the chief classes of Hindus in Bombay.

disbandment in 1679, in pursuance of Sir Josia Child's ill-conceived policy of retrenchment: but as the orders for its abolition arrived at the very moment when Sivaji was threatening a descent on Bombay and the Sidi was flouting the Company's authority and seizing their territory, even the subservient John Child could not face the risk involved in carrying out the instructions from home; and in the following year the orders were rescinded.[1] The force, however, did not wholly escape the consequences of Child's cheese-paring policy. By the end of 1682 there was only one ensign for the whole force of 500, and of non-commissioned officers there were only three sergeants and two corporals. Nevertheless the times were so troubled that they had to remain continuously under arms.[2] It is therefore not surprising that when Keigwin raised the standard of revolt against the Company in December 1683, the militia sided in a body with him and his fellow-mutineers, and played an active part in the bloodless revolution which they achieved. Two years after the restoration of Bombay to Sir Thomas Grantham, who had been commissioned by the Company to secure the surrender of Keigwin and his associates, a further reference to the militia appears in an order of November 15th, 1686, by Sir John Wyborne, Deputy Governor, to John Wyat.[3] The latter was instructed to repair to Sewri with two topasses and take charge of a new guard-house, to allow no runaway soldiers or others to leave the island, to prevent cattle, corn or provisions being taken out of Bombay, and to arrest and search any person carrying letters and send him to the Deputy Governor. The order concluded with the following words:—

> "Suffer poor people to come and inhabit on the island; *and call the militia to watch with you every night,* sparing the Padre of Parel's servants."

1. R. and O. Strachey, *Keigwin's Rebellion,* p. 41.
2. Ibid. p. 68.
3. Bombay Gazetteer, Vol. XXVI. (Materials), Part III, p. 8.

The terms of the order indicate to some extent the dangers and difficulties which confronted Bombay at this epoch: and it is a reasonable inference that the duties of the militia were dictated mainly by the military and political exigencies of a period in which the hostility of the neighbouring powers in Western India and serious internal troubles produced a constant series of "alarums and excursions".

The close of the seventeenth and the earlier years of the eighteenth century were marked by much lawlessness; and in the outlying parts of Bombay the militia appears to have formed the only safeguard of the residents against robbery and violence. This is clear from an order of September 13, 1694, addressed by Sir John Gayer, the Governor, to Jansanay (Janu Shenvi) Subehdar of Worli, Ramaji Avdat, Subehdar of Mahim, Raji Karga, Subehdar of Sion, and Bodji Patan, Subehdar of Sewri. "Being informed," he wrote, "that certain ill people on this island go about in the night to the number of ten or twelve or more, designing some mischief or disturbance to the inhabitants, these are to enorder you to go the rounds every night with twenty men at all places which you think most suitable to intercept such persons."[1] The strengthening of the force at this period[2] and the increased activity of the night-patrols had very little effect in reducing the volume of crime, which was a natural consequence of the general weakness of the administration. The appalling mortality among Europeans, the lack of discipline among the soldiers of the garrison, the general immorality to which Ovington, the chaplain, bore witness,[3] the prevalence of piracy and the lack of proper laws and legal machinery, all contributed to render Bombay "very unhealthful" and to offer unlimited scope to the lawless section of the population.

1. Bombay Gazetteer, Vol. XXVI, Part iii, p. 8.
2. Gazetteer of Bombay City and Island, Vol. II, p. 238.
3. Rev. F. Ovington, *Voyage to Suratt in 1689*. London, 1696.

As regards the law, judicial functions were exercised at the beginning of the eighteenth century by a civil officer of the Company, styled Chief Justice, and in important cases by the President in Council. Neither of these officials had any real knowledge of law; no codes existed, except two rough compilations made during Aungier's governorship: and justice was consequently very arbitrary. In 1726 this Court was exercising civil, criminal, military, admiralty and probate jurisdiction; it also framed rules for the price of bread and the wages of "black tailors".[1] Connected with the Court from 1720 to 1727 were the *Vereadores*,[2] a body of native functionaries who looked after orphans and the estates of persons dying intestate, and audited accounts. After 1726 they also exercised minor judicial powers and seem to have partly taken the place of the native tribunals, which up to 1696 administered justice to the Indian inhabitants of the Island.[3] So matters remained until 1726, when under the Charter creating Mayors' Courts at Calcutta, Bombay and Madras the Governor and Council were empowered to hold quarter sessions for the trial of all offences except high treason, the President and the five senior members of Council being created Justices of the Peace and constituting a Court of Oyer and Terminer and Gaol Delivery.

For purposes of criminal justice Bombay was considered a county. The curious state of the law at this date is apparent from the trial of a woman, named Gangi, who was indicted in 1744 for petty treason in aiding and abetting one Vitha Bhandari in the murder of her husband.[4] She was found guilty and was sentenced to be burnt. Apparently the penalty for compassing a

1. P. B. Malabari, *Bombay in the Making*, p. 437.
2. Ibid. p. 465. *Vereador* means procurator or attorney. The *Vereador* wore a gown as Vereador da Camera or member of a town council (Da Cunha).
3. Gazetteer of Bombay City and Island, Vol. II, p. 212.
4. Bombay Gazetteer, Vol. XXVI, Part iii, pp. 8 ff.

husband's death was the same as for high treason: and the sentence of burning for petty treason was the only sentence the Court could legally have passed. Twenty years earlier (1724) an ignorant woman, by name Bastok, was accused of witchcraft and other "diabolical practices." The Court found her guilty, not from evil intent, but on account of ignorance, and sentenced her to receive eleven lashes at the church door and afterwards to do penance in the building.[1]

The system, whereby criminal jurisdiction was vested in the Governor and Council, lasted practically till the close of the eighteenth century. In 1753, for example, the Bombay Government was composed of the Governor and thirteen councillors, all of whom were Justices of the Peace and Commissioners of Oyer and Terminer and Gaol Delivery. They were authorised to hold quarter sessions and make bye-laws for the good government etc. of Bombay: and to aid them in the exercise of their magisterial powers as Justices, they had an executive officer, the Sheriff, with a very limited establishment.[2] In 1757 and 1759 they issued proclamations embodying various "rules for the maintenance of the peace and comfort of Bombay's inhabitants"; but with the possible exception of the Sheriff, they had no executive agency to enforce the observance of these rules and bye-laws, and no body of men, except the militia, for the prevention and detection of offences. When, therefore, in 1769 the state of the public security called loudly for reform, the Bombay Government were forced to content themselves and their critics with re-publishing these various proclamations and regulations—a course which, as may be supposed, effected very little real good. In a letter to the Court of Directors, dated December 20th, 1769, they reported that in consequence

1. P. B. Malabari, *Bombay in the Making*, p. 287.
2. Warden's Report in W. H. Morley, *Analytical Digest of Cases decided in the Supreme Court of Judicature* (London, 1849), Vol. II, p. 458.

of a letter from a bench of H. M.'s Justices they had issued on August 26, 1769, "sundry regulations for the better conducting the police of the place in general, particularly in respect to the markets for provisions of every kind"; and these regulations were in due course approved by the Court in a dispatch of April 25, 1771.[1]

Police arrangements, however, were still very unsatisfactory, and crimes of violence, murder and robbery were so frequent outside the town walls that in August, 1771, Brigadier-General David Wedderburn[2] submitted proposals to the Bombay Government for rendering the Bhandari militia[3], as it was then styled, more efficient. His plan may be said to mark the definite employment of the old militia on regular police duties. Accordingly the Bombay Bhandaris were formed into a battalion composed of 48 officers and 400 men, which furnished nightly a guard of 12 officers and 100 men "for the protection of the woods." This guard was distributed as follows:—

4 officers and 33 men at Washerman's Tank (Dhobi Talao)
4 " " 33 " near Major Mace's house.
4 " " 34 " at Mamba Davy (Mumbadevi) tank.

From these posts constant patrols, which were in communication with one another, were sent out from dark until gunfire in the morning, the whole area between Dongri and Back Bay being thus covered during the night. The *Vereadores* were instructed to appoint not less than 20 trusty and respectable Portuguese *fazendars* to attend singly or in pairs every night at the various police posts.

1. W. H. Morley, *Digest etc*, Vol. II (Warden's Report); Bombay Gazetteer, Vol. XXVI, iii.
2. General Wedderburn was killed at the storming of Broach in November, 1772.
3. The fact that it was called the Bhandari militia implies that the Native Christian element had largely disappeared, and that Bhandaris and other Hindus of the lower classes formed the bulk of the force.

All Europeans living in Sonapur or Dongri had to obtain passes according to their class, *i. e.* those in the marine forces from the Superintendent, those in the military forces from their commanding officer, all other Europeans, not in the Company's service, but living in Bombay by permission of the Government, from the Secretary to Government, and all artificers employed in any of the offices from the head of their office.

The duties of the patrols were to keep the peace, to seize all persons found rioting, pending examination, to arrest all robbers and housebreakers, to seize all Europeans without passes, and all *coffrees* (African slaves) found in greater numbers than two together, or armed with swords, sticks, knives or bludgeons. All *coffrees* or other runaway slaves were to be apprehended, and were punished by being put to work on the fortifications for a year at a wage of Rs. 3 per month, or by being placed aboard cruisers for the same term, a notice being published of their age, size, country of origin and description, so that their masters might have a chance of claiming them. If unclaimed by the end of twelve months, they were shipped to Bencoolen in Sumatra.

The standing order to all persons to register their slaves was to be renewed and enforced under a penalty. The Company agreed to pay the Bhandari police Rs. 10 for every *coffree* or runaway slave arrested and placed on the works or on a cruiser; Re. 1 for every slave absent from his work for three days; and Rs. 2 for every slave absent from duty for one month; Re. 1 for every soldier or sailor absent from duty for forty-eight hours, whom they might arrest; and 8 annas for every soldier or sailor found drunk in the woods after 8 p. m. The money earned in the latter cases was to be paid at once by the Marine Superintendent or the Commanding Officer, as the case might be, and deducted from the pay of the defaulter; and the total sum thus collected was to be divided once a month or oftener among the Bhandaris on duty.

Armed Police Constable
Bombay City

The officers in charge of the police posts and the Portuguese *fazendars*, attached thereto, were to make a daily report of all that had happened during the night and place all persons arrested by the patrols before a magistrate for examination. The Bhandari patrols were to assemble daily at 5 p. m. opposite to the Church Gate (of the Fort) and, weather permitting, they were to be taught "firing motions and the platoon exercise, and to fire balls at a mark, for which purpose some good havaldars should attend to instruct them, and the adjutant of the day or some other European officer should constantly attend."

These Bhandari night-patrols, as organized by General Wedderburn, were the germ from which sprang the later police administration of the Island. We see the beginnings of police sections and divisions in the three main night-posts with their complement of officers and men; the forerunner of the modern divisional morning report in the daily report of the patrol officer and the *fazendar;* and the establishment of an armed branch in the fire-training given to the patrols in the evening. The presence of the *fazendars* was probably based on the occasional need of an interpreter and of having some advisory check upon the exercise of their powers by the patrols. In those early days the *fazendar* may have supplied the place of public opinion, which now plays no unimportant part in the police administration of the modern city.

Notwithstanding these arrangements, the volume of crime showed no diminution. Murder, robbery and theft were still of frequent occurrence outside the Fort walls: and in the vain hope of imposing some check upon the lawless element, the Bombay Government in August, 1776, ordered parties of regular sepoys to be added to the Bhandari patrols. Three years later, in February, 1779, they decided, apparently as an experiment, to supplant the Bhandari militia entirely by patrols of sepoys, which were to be furnished by "the battalion of sepoy marines". These patrols were to scour the woods nightly, accompanied by "a peace officer", who was to report every morning to the acting magistrate.[1] Still there was no improvement, and the dissatisfaction of the general public was forcibly expressed at the close of 1778 or early in the following year by the grand Jury, which demanded a thorough reform of the police.[2] In the course of their presentment they stated that "the frequent robberies and the difficulties attending the detection of aggressors, called loudly for some establishment clothed with such authority as should effectually protect the innocent and bring the guilty to trial", and they proposed that His Majesty's Justices should apply to Government for the appointment of an officer with ample authority to effect the end in view.[3]

This pronouncement of the Grand Jury was the precursor of the first appointment of an executive Chief of Police in Bombay. On February 17, 1779, Mr. James Tod (or Todd) was appointed "Lieutenant of Police", on probation, with an allowance of Rs. 4 per diem, and on March 3rd of that year he was sworn into office; a formal commission signed by Mr. William Hornby, the Governor, was granted to him, and a public notification of the creation of the office and of the powers vested in it was issued. He was also furnished with copies of the regulations in force, and was required by the terms of his commission to follow all orders given to him by the Government or by the Justices of the Peace.[4]

Tod had a chequered career as head of the Bombay police. The first attack upon him was delivered by the very body which had urged the creation of his appointment. The Grand Jury, like the frogs of Æsop who demanded a King, found the appointment little to their liking, and were moved in the following July (1779) to present "the

1. Bombay Gazetteer, Vol. XXVI (Materials), Part iii.
2. Morley *Digest* etc. (Warden's Report).
3. Ibid.
4. Ibid. Bombay Gazetteer, Vol. XXVI, Part iii.

said James Todd as a public nuisance, and his office of Police as of a most dangerous tendency"; and they earnestly recommended "that it be immediately abolished, as fit only for a despotic government, where a Bastille is at hand to enforce its authority".

The Government very properly paid no heed to this curious *volteface* of the Grand Jury, and Tod was left free to draft a new set of police regulations, which were badly needed, and to do what he could to bring his force of militia into shape. His regulations were submitted on December 31, 1779, and were approved by the Bombay Council and ordered to be published on January 26th, 1780. They were based upon notifications and orders previously issued from time to time at the Presidency and approved by the Justices, and were eventually registered in the Court of Oyer and Terminer and Gaol Delivery on April 17, 1780. Between the date of their approval by the Council and their registration by the Court, Tod revised them on the lines of the Police regulations adopted in Calcutta in 1778.[1] It was further provided at the time of their registration that "a Bench of Justices during the recess of the Sessions should be authorized from time to time to make any necessary alterations and amendments in the code, subject to their being affirmed or reversed at the General Quarter Sessions of the Peace next ensuing". Tod's regulations, which numbered forty-one, were the only rules for the management of the police which had been passed up to that date in a formal manner. They were first approved in Council, as mentioned above, by the authority of the Royal Charter of 1753, granted to the East India Company, and were then published and registered at the Sessions under the authority conveyed by the subsequent Act (13 Geo. III) of 1773. They thus constituted the earliest Bombay Police Code.

1. At that date the office of Superintendent of Police existed at Calcutta.

Meanwhile Tod found his new post by no means a bed of roses. On November 30th, 1779, he wrote to the Council stating that his work as Lieutenant of Police had created for him many enemies and difficulties. He had twice been indicted for felony and had been honourably acquitted on both occasions: but he still lived in continual dread of blame. "By unremitting and persevering attention to duty I have made many and bitter enemies", he wrote, "in consequence of which I have been obliged in great measure to give up my bread." He added that his military title of Lieutenant of Police had proved obnoxious to many, and he offered to resign it, suggesting at the same time that, following the precedent set by Calcutta, he should be styled Superintendent of Police. Lastly he asked the Council to fix his emoluments. The censure of the Grand Jury, quoted in a previous paragraph, indicates clearly the opposition with which Tod was faced; and one cannot but sympathize with an officer whose endeavours to perform his duty efficiently resulted in his arraignment before a criminal court. That he was honourably acquitted on both occasions shows that at this date at any rate he was the victim of malicious persecution.

As regards the style and title of his appointment, the Bombay Council endorsed his views, and on March 29th, 1780, they declared the office of Lieutenant of Police annulled, and created in its place the office of Deputy of Police on a fixed salary of Rs. 3,000 a year. Accordingly on April 5th, 1780, Tod formally relinquished his former office and was appointed Deputy of Police, being permitted to draw his salary of Rs. 3,000 a year with retrospective effect from the date of his first appointment as "Lieutenant". On the same day he submitted the revised code of police regulations, which was formally registered in the Court of Oyer and Terminer on April 17th. In abolishing the post of Lieutenant the Bombay Government anticipated by a few months the order of the Court of Directors, who wrote as follows on July 5th, 1780:—

> "Determined as we are to resist every attempt that may be made to create new offices at the expense of the Company, we cannot but be highly displeased with your having appointed an officer in quality of Lieutenant of Police with a salary of Rs. 4 a day. Whatever sum may have been paid in consequence must be refunded. If such an officer be of that utility to the public as you have represented, the public by some tax or otherwise should defray the charges thereof."

Before leaving the subject of the actual appointment, it is to be noted that at some date previous to 1780 the office of High Constable was annexed to that of Deputy of Police; for, in his letter to the Court of Sessions asking for the confirmation and publication of his police regulations, Tod describes himself as "Deputy of Police and High Constable". No information, however, is forthcoming as to when this office was created, nor when it was amalgamated with the appointment of Deputy of Police.[1]

The actual details of Tod's police administration are obscure. At the outset he was apparently hampered by lack of funds, for which the Bombay Government had made no provision. On January 17th, 1780, he submitted to them an account of sums which he had advanced and expended in pursuance of his duties as executive head of the police, and also informed the Council that twenty-four constables, "who had been sworn in for the villages without the gates", had received no pay and consequently had, in concert with the Bhandaris, been exacting heavy fees from the inhabitants. Tod requested the Government to pay the wages due to these men, or, failing that, to authorize payment by a general assessment on all heads of families residing outside the gates of the town. The Council reimbursed Tod's expenses

1. Gazetteer of Bombay City and Island, Vol. II, p. 241 (note) Morley, *Digest etc.*

and issued orders for an assessment to meet the cost of the constabulary.

While allowing for the many difficulties confronting him, Tod cannot be held to have achieved much success as head of the police. His old critics, the Grand Jury, returned to the charge at the Sessions which opened on April 30th, 1787, and protested in strong terms against "the yet inefficient state of every branch of the Police, which required immediate and effectual amendment". "That part of it" they said, "which had for its object the personal security of the inhabitants and their property was not sufficiently vigorous to prevent the frequent repetition of murder, felony, and every other species of atrociousness—defects that had often been the subject of complaint from the Grand Jury of Bombay, but never with more reason than at that Sessions, as the number of prisoners for various offences bore ample testimony."

They animadverted on the want of proper regulations, on the great difficulty of obtaining menial servants and the still greater difficulty of retaining them in their service, on the enormous wages which they demanded and their generally dubious characters. So far as concerned the domestic servant problem, the Bombay public at the close of the eighteenth century seems to have been in a position closely resembling that of the middle-classes in England at the close of the Great War (1914–18). The Grand Jury complained also of the defective state of the high roads, of the uncleanliness of many streets in the Town, and of "the filthiness of some of the inhabitants, being uncommonly offensive and a real nuisance to society". They objected to the obstruction caused by the piling of cotton on the Green and in the streets, to the enormous price of the necessaries of life, the bad state of the markets, and the high rates of labour. They urged the Justices to press the Bombay Government for reform and suggested "the appointment of a Committee of Police with full powers to frame regulations and armed with sufficient authority to carry them into execution, as had already been done with happy effect on the representation of the Grand Juries at the other Presidencies."

The serious increase of robbery and "nightly depredations" was ascribed chiefly to the fact that all persons were allowed to enter Bombay freely, without examination, and that the streets were infested with beggars "calling themselves Faquiers and Jogees (Fakirs and Jogis)", who exacted contributions from the public. The beggar-nuisance is one of the chief problems requiring solution in the modern City of Bombay: and it may be some consolation to a harassed Commissioner of Police to know that his predecessor of the eighteenth century was faced with similar difficulties. The Grand Jury were not over-squeamish in their recommendations on the subject. They advocated the immediate deportation of all persons having no visible means of subsistence, and as a result the police, presumably under Tod's orders, sent thirteen suspicious persons out of the Island.[1]

Three years later, in 1790, Tod's administration came to a disastrous close. He was tried for corruption. "The principal witness against him (as must always happen)", wrote Sir James Mackintosh, "was his native receiver of bribes. He expatiated on the danger to all Englishmen of convicting them on such testimony; but in spite of a topic which, by declaring all black agents incredible, would render all white villains secure, he was convicted; though—too lenient a judgment—he was only reprimanded and suffered to resign his station".[2] Sir James Mackintosh, as is clear from his report of October, 1811, to the Bombay Government, was stoutly opposed to the system of granting the chief executive police officer wide judicial powers, such as those exercised by Tod and his immediate successors: and his hostility to the system may

1. Morley, *Digest etc.* (Warden's Report) Vol. II; Bombay Gazetteer, Vol. XXVI, Part III, 67.
2. Sir J. Mackintosh's letter in Morley, *Digest etc.*, Vol. II, p. 513.

have led to his overlooking the exceptional difficulties and temptations to which Tod was exposed. The Governor and his three Councillors, in whom by Act XXIV, Geo. III, of 1785 ("for the better regulation and management of the affairs of the East India Company and for establishing a Court of Judicature"), the supreme judicial and executive administration of Bombay were at this date vested, realized perhaps that Tod's emoluments of Rs. 250 a month were scarcely large enough to secure the integrity of an official vested with such wide powers over a community, whose moral standards were admittedly low, that Tod had done a certain amount of good work under difficult conditions, and that the very nature of his office was bound to create him many enemies. On these considerations they may have deemed it right to temper justice with mercy and to permit the delinquent to resign his appointment in lieu of being dismissed.

The identity of Tod's immediate successor is unknown. Whoever he was, he seems to have effected no amelioration of existing conditions. In 1793 the Grand Jury again drew pointed attention to "the total inadequacy of the police arrangements for the preservation of the peace and the prevention of crimes, and for bringing criminals to justice." Bombay was the scene of constant robberies by armed gangs, none of whom were apprehended. The close of the eighteenth century was a period of chaos and internecine warfare throughout a large part of India, and it is only natural that Bombay should have suffered to some extent from the inroads of marauders, tempted by the prospect of loot. A system of night-patrols, weak in numbers and poorly paid, could not grapple effectively with organized gangs of free-booters, nurtured on dangerous enterprises and accustomed to great rapidity of movement. The complaints of the Grand Jury, however, could not be overlooked, and led directly to the appointment of a committee to consider the whole subject of the police administration and suggest reform.

This committee was in the midst of its enquiry when Act XXXIII, Geo. III. of 1793 was promulgated and rendered further investigation unnecessary. Under that Act a Commission of the Peace, based upon the form adopted in England, was issued for each Presidency by the Supreme Court of Judicature in Bengal. The Governor and his Councillors remained *ex officiis* Justices of the Peace for the Island, and five additional Justices were appointed by the Governor-General-in-Council on the recommendation of the Bombay Government. The Commission of the Peace further provided for the abolition of the office of Deputy of Police and High Constable, and created in its place the office of Superintendent of Police.

The first Superintendent of Police was Mr. Simon Halliday, who just prior to the promulgation of the Act above-mentioned had been nominated by the Justices to the office of High Constable. So much appears from the records of the Court of Sessions; and one may presume that after the Act came into operation in 1793 Mr. Halliday's title was altered to that of Superintendent. His powers were somewhat curtailed to accord with the powers vested in the Superintendent of Police at Calcutta, and he was bound to keep the Governor-in-Council regularly informed of all action taken by him in his official capacity.

Mr. Halliday was in charge of the office of Superintendent of Police until 1808. His assumption of office synchronized with a thorough revision of the arrangements for policing the area outside the Fort, which up to that date had proved wholly ineffective. Under the new system, which is stated in Warden's Report to have been introduced in 1793 and was approved by the Justices a little later, the troublesome area known as "Dungree and the Woods" was split up into 14 police divisions, each division being staffed by 2 Constables (European) and a varying number of Peons (not exceeding 130 for the whole area), who were to be stationary in their respective charges and responsible for dealing with all illegal acts committed within their limits.

The disposition of this force of 158 men was as follows:—

Name of Chokey	Number of Constables	Number of Peons	Total
Washerman's Tank (Dhobi Talao).	2	12	14
Back Bay	2	10	12
Palo (Apollo *i. e.* Girgaum Road).	2	6	8
Girgen (Girgaum)	2	12	14
Gowdevy (Gamdevi)	2	8	10
Pillajee Ramjee[1]	2	8	10
Moomladevy (Mumbadevi) ...	2	10	12
Calvadevy (Kalbadevi)	2	8	10
Sheik Maymon's Market (Sheik Memon Street ?) ...	2	10	12
Butchers (Market ?)	2	10	12
Cadjees (Kazi's market or post) ...	2	8	10
Ebram Cowns (Ibrahim Khan's market or post).	2	8	10
Sat Tar (Sattad Street)	2	12	14
Portuguese Church (Cavel) ...	2	8	10
	28	130	158

The names of the police-stations or *chaukis* (chokeys) show that the area thus policed included roughly the modern Dhobi Talao section and the southern part of Girgaum, most of the present Market and Bhuleshwar sections and the western parts of the modern Dongri and Mandvi sections. In fact, the expression "Dongri and the Woods" represented the area which formed the nucleus of what were known in the middle of the nine-

1. It is not clear whether this post is identical with "Pilaji Ramji's Naka" of the twentieth century, which is the name familiarly applied to the junction of Grant Road and Duncan Road near the Northbrook Gardens. Here some years ago one Pilaji Ramji occupied a corner house, in which he used to place an enormous figure of the god Ganesh during the annual Ganpati festival. Large crowds of Hindus used to visit the house to see the idol, and hence gave the name "Pilaji's post" to the locality. It is quite possible that the name first came into use in the eighteenth century.

teenth century as the "Old Town" and "New Town". At the date of Mr. Halliday's appointment, this part of the Island was almost entirely covered with oarts (*hortas*) and plantations, intersected by a few narrow roads; and if one may judge by the illustration "A Night in Dongri" in *The Adventures of Qui-hi* (1816),[1] a portion of this area was inhabited largely by disreputable persons.

Simultaneously with the introduction of the arrangements described above, an establishment of "rounds" hitherto maintained by the arrack-farmer, consisting of one clerk of militia, 4 havaldars and 86 sepoys, and costing Rs. 318 per month, was abolished. Mahim, which was still regarded as a suburb, had its own "Chief," who performed general, magisterial and police duties in that area; while other outlying places like Sion and Sewri were furnished with a small body of native police under a native officer, subject to the general supervision and control of the Superintendent. In 1797 the condition of the public thoroughfares and roads was so bad that, on the death in that year of Mr. Lankhut, the Surveyor of Roads, his department was placed in charge of the Superintendent of Police; while in 1800 the office of Clerk of the Market was also annexed to that of the chief police officer, in pursuance of the recommendations of a special committee. In the following year, 1801, the old office of Chief of Mahim was finally abolished, and his magisterial and police duties were thereupon vested in the Superintendent of Police. To enable him to cope with this additional duty, an appointment of Deputy Superintendent, officiating in the Mahim district, was created, the holder of which was directly subordinate in all matters to the Superintendent of Police. The first Deputy Superintendent was Mr. James Fisher, who continued in office until the date (1808) of Mr. Halliday's retirement when he was succeeded by Mr. James Morley.

1. Published in 1816, with illustrations by Rowlandson.

CHAPTER II

THE RISE OF THE MAGISTRACY
1800—1855

As has been shown in the preceding chapter, the importance of the office of Superintendent of Police had been considerably enhanced by the year 1809. Excluding the control of markets and roads, which was taken from him in that year, the Superintendent had executive control of all police arrangements in the Island, exercised all the duties of a High Constable, an Alderman and a Justice of the Peace, was Secretary of the Committee of Buildings, a member of the Town Committee, and a member of the Buildings Committee of H.M.'s Naval Offices in Bombay. He had been appointed a Justice of the Peace at his own request, on the grounds that he would thereby be enabled to carry out his police work more effectively. His deputy at Mahim was also appointed a Justice of the Peace on the publication of Act XLVIII, Geo. III. of 1808.

The year 1809 marks another crisis in the history of Bombay's police administration, to which several factors may be held to have contributed. In the first place crime was still rampant and defied all attempts to reduce it. Bodies of armed men continued to enter the Island, as for example in 1806 and 1807, and to terrify, molest and loot the residents; and though these gangs remained for some little time within the Superintendent's jurisdiction, they were never apprehended by the police.[1] In his report of November 15, 1810, Warden refers also to an attack by "Cossids", *i. e. Kasids* or letter-carriers, who must have been induced to leave for the moment their ordinary duties as postal-runners and messengers by the apparent immunity from arrest and punishment

1 Morley, *Digest etc.* (Warden's Report), Vol. II, p. 492.

enjoyed by the bands of regular thieves and freebooters. In consequence of the general lawlessness traffic in stolen goods was at this date a most lucrative profession, and obliged the Justices in 1797 to nominate individual goldsmiths and *shroffs* as public pawnbrokers for a term of five years, on condition that they gave security for good conduct and furnished the police regularly with returns of valuable goods sold or purchased by them.[1] Another source of annoyance to the authorities was the constant desertion of sailors from the vessels of the Royal Navy and of the East India Company. These men were rarely arrested and the police appeared unable to discover their haunts. The peons, *i.e.* native constables were declared to be seldom on duty, except when they expected the Superintendent to pass, and to spend their time generally in gambling and other vices. In brief, the police force was so inefficient and crime was so widespread and uncontrolled that public opinion demanded urgent reform.

In the second place, the old system whereby the Governor and his Council constituted the Court of Oyer and Terminer and Gaol Delivery disappeared on the establishment in 1798 of a Recorder's Court. The powers of the Justices, who were authorized to hold Sessions of the Peace, remained unimpaired, and nine of them, exclusive of the Members of Government, were nominated for the Town and Island. It was inevitable that the constitution of a competent judicial tribunal, presided over by a trained lawyer, should, apart from other causes, lead to a general stock-taking of the judicial administration of Bombay, and incidentally should direct increased attention to the subject of the powers vested in the Police and the source whence they drew their authority.

The powers of the Superintendent of Police at this epoch were very wide. First, he had power to convict offenders summarily and punish them at the police office.

1. *Bombay Courier*, February 4th, 1797.

This procedure, in the opinion of the Recorder, Sir James Mackintosh (1803-11), was quite illegal, inasmuch as the punishments were inflicted under rules, which from 1753 to 1807 were not confirmed by the Court of Directors and had therefore no validity. The rules made between 1807 and 1811 were likewise declared by the same authority to be invalid, as they had not been registered in the court of judicature. On other grounds also the police rules authorizing this procedure were *ultra vires.* Secondly, the Superintendent inflicted the punishment of banishment and condemned offenders to hard labour in chains on public works. Between February 28, 1808, and January 31, 1809, he (*i.e.* Mr. Halliday) banished 217 persons from Bombay, and condemned 64 persons to hard labour in the docks. During the three years, 1807-1809, about 200 offenders were thus condemned to work in chains. On the other hand, the Superintendent frequently liberated prisoners before the expiry of their sentence, and in this way released 26 persons on December 20, 1809, without assigning any reason. He condemned persons also to flogging. He kept *no* record of his cases. "He may arrest 40 men in the morning", wrote Sir James Mackintosh, "he may try, convict and condemn them in the forenoon; and he may close the day by exercising the Royal prerogative of pardon towards them all." It is hardly surprising that the mind of the lawyer revolted against the system, and that in his indignation he characterized the powers of the Superintendent as "a precipitate, clandestine and arbitrary jurisdiction."[1]

In the third place, the powers of the Governor-in-Council to enact police regulations for Bombay were defined anew and enlarged by Act XLVII, Geo. III. of 1808, under the provisions of which the Government was empowered to nominate 16 persons, exclusive of the members of the Governor's Council, to act as Justices of the Peace. The promulgation of this Act, which was

1. Sir J. Mackintosh's letter of October, 1811, in Morley, *Digest etc.* Vol. II.

received in Bombay in 1808, rendered necessary a thorough revision of the conditions and circumstances of police control.

In consequence, therefore, of the prevalence of crime and the notorious inefficiency and corruption of the Police, the hostility of the new Recorder's Court to the existing system of administration, and the need of a new enactment under Act XLVII, the Bombay Government appointed a committee in 1809 to review the whole position and make suggestions for further reform. The President of the committee was Mr. F. Warden, Chief Secretary to Government, who eventually submitted proposals in a letter dated November 15, 1810. The urgent need of reform was emphasized by the fact that the Superintendent of Police, Mr. Charles Briscoe, who had succeeded Mr. Halliday in 1809, was tried at the Sessions of November, 1810, for corruption, as Tod had been in 1790, and that complaints against the tyranny and inefficiency of the force were being daily received by the authorities. Sir James Mackintosh was only expressing public opinion when in 1811 he recommended Government "in their wisdom and justice to abolish even the name of Superintendent of Police, and to efface every vestige of an office of which no enlightened friend to the honour of the British name can recollect the existence without pain."

Warden's proposals were briefly the following. He advocated the adaptation to Bombay of Colquhoun's system for improving the police of London, and suggested the appointment on fixed salaries of two executive magistrates for the criminal branch of the Police, to be selected from among the Company's servants or British subjects—, "one for the Town of Bombay, whose jurisdiction shall extend to the Engineer's limits and to Colaba, and to offences committed in the harbour of Bombay, with a suitable establishment; and a second for the division without the garrison, including the district of Mahim, with a suitable establishment." Both these magistrates were to have executive and judicial functions, and were also to perform "municipal duties".[1] The active functions of the police were to be performed by a Deputy, while "the control, influence, and policy" were to be centred in a Superintendent-General of Police, aided by the two magistrates. The latter officer was to be responsible for the recruitment of the Deputy's subordinates, and the *Mukadams* (headmen) of each caste were to form part of the police establishment.

Warden dealt at some length with the qualifications and powers which the chief police officer should possess. He proposed that the Superintendent's power of inflicting corporal punishment should be abolished, and that his duties should extend only to the apprehension, not to the punishment, of offenders; to the enforcement of regulations for law and order; to the superintendence of the scavenger's and road-repairing departments; to watching "the motley group of characters that infest this populous island;" and to the vigilant supervision of houses maintained for improper and illegal purposes. "He should be the arbitrator of disputes between the natives, arising out of their religious prejudices. He should have authority over the Harbour, and should be in charge of convicts subjected to hard labour in the Docks, and those sent down to Bombay under sentence of transportation. He should not be the whole day closeted in his chamber, but abroad and active in the discharge of his duty; he should now and then appear where least expected. The power and vital influence of the office, and not its name only, should be known and felt. He ought to number among his acquaintances every rogue in the place and know all their haunts and movements. A character of this description is not imaginary, nor difficult of formation. We have heard of a Sartine and a Fouché; a Colquhoun exists; and I am informed that the character of Mr. Blaqueire at Calcutta, as a Magistrate, is equally efficient." Warden, indeed,

1. Warden's Report in Morley, *Digest etc.* Vol. II, pp. 482 ff.

demanded a kind of "admirable Crichton,"—strictly honest, yet the boon-companion of every rascal in Bombay, keeping abreast of his office-work by day and perambulating the more dangerous haunts of the local criminals by night. It is only on rare occasions that a man of such varied abilities and energy is forthcoming: and nearly half a century was destined to elapse before Bombay found a Police Superintendent who more than fulfilled the high standard recommended by the Chief Secretary in 1810.

The upshot of the Police Committee's enquiry and of the report of its President was the publication of Rule, Ordinance and Regulation I of 1812, which was drafted by Sir James Mackintosh in 1811, and formed the basis of the police administration of Bombay until 1856. Under this Regulation, three Justices of the Peace were appointed Magistrates of Police with the following respective areas of jurisdiction:—

(*a*) The Senior Magistrate, for the Fort and Harbour.

(*b*) The Second Magistrate, for the area between the Fort Walls and a line drawn from the northern boundary of Mazagon to Breach Candy.

(*c*) The Third Magistrate, with his office at Mahim, for all the rest of the Island.[1]

Included in the official staff of these three magistrates were:—

a Purvoe (*i. e.* Prabhu clerk)		on Rs. 50 per month
a Cauzee (Kazi)	... ...	" " 8 " "
a Bhut (Bhat, Brahman)	...	" " 8 " "
a Jew Cauzee (Rabbi)	...	" " 12 " "
an Andaroo (Parsi Mobed)	...	" " 6 " "
Two Constables	... each	" " 9 " "
One Havildar	... ...	" " 8 " "
Four Peons	... ... each	" " 6 " "

1. The Third Magistrate was not appointed until 1830. The other two were appointed in 1812, and the Second exercised jurisdiction over the whole Island, excluding the Fort and Harbour.

The executive head of the Police force was a Deputy of Police and High Constable on a salary of Rs. 500 a month, while the general control and deliberative powers were vested in a Superintendent-General of Police. All appointments of individuals to the subordinate ranks of the force were made by the Magistrates of Police, who with the Superintendent-General met regularly as a Bench to consider all matters appertaining to the police administration of Bombay. European constables were appointed by the Justices at Quarter Sessions, and the *Mukadams* or headmen of each caste formed an integral feature of the police establishment.

The strength and cost of the force in 1812 were as follows :—

1	Deputy of Police and Head Constable	Rs. 500 per month
2	European Assistants (at Rs. 100 each)	Rs. 200 " "
3	Purvoes (Prabhus, clerks) ...	Rs. 110 " "
1	Inspector of Markets	Rs. 80 " "
2	Overseers of Roads (respectable natives at 50 each)	Rs. 100 " "
12	Havaldars (at Rs. 8 each) ...	Rs. 96 " "
8	Naiks (at Rs. 7 each)... ...	Rs. 56 " "
6	European Constables... ...	Rs. 365 " "
50	Peons (at Rs. 6 each)... ...	Rs. 300 " "
1	Battaki man	Rs. 6 " "
1	Havaldar and 12 Peons for the Mahim patrol	Rs. 80 " "
Harbour Police.		
7	Boats *i.e.* 49 men	Rs. 300 " "
1	Purvoe	Rs. 50 " "
4	Peons (at Rs. 6 each)	Rs. 24 " "
	Contingencies	Rs. 74 " "

Thus, including the Deputy of Police, the land force comprised 10 Europeans, one of whom was in charge of the markets, and 86 Indians, of whom two were inspectors of roads. The clerical staff consisted of three Prabhus. The water-police consisted of 53 Indians and one clerk. The cost of the force, including the water-police, amounted to Rs. 27,204 a year, to which had to be added Rs. 888 for contingencies, Rs. 1425 for the clothing of havaldars and peons, and Rs. 2000 for stationery.[1]

The inclusion in the magisterial establishment of "a Cauzee" etc. requires brief comment. Down to 1790 the administration of criminal justice in India was largely in the hands of Indian judges and officials of various denominations, though under European supervision in various forms; and even after that date, when the native judiciary had ceased to exist except in quite subordinate positions, the law that was administered in criminal cases was in substance Muhammadan law, and a Kazi and a Mufti were retained in the provincial courts of appeal and circuit as the exponents of Muhammadan law and the deliverers of a formal *fatwa*. The term Kazi on this account remained in formal existence till the abolition of the Sadr Courts in 1862.[2] The object of associating Kazis with the Bombay magistrates of police at the opening of the nineteenth century was doubtless to ensure that in all cases brought before them, involving questions of the law, customs and traditions of the chief communities and sects inhabiting the Island, the magistrates should have the advantage of consulting those who were able to interpret and give a ruling on such matters. The Kazi proper was the authority on all matters relating to the Muhammadan community; the "Jew Cauzee" on matters relating to the Bene-Israel, who from 1760 to the middle of the nineteenth century contributed an important element to the Company's military forces;[3] the Bhat presumably gave advice on

1. Morley, *Digest etc.* (Warden's Report), Vol. II.
2. Hobson-Jobson, 1903, s. v. Cazee.
3. The Kazis of the Bene-Israel officiated at all festivals of the community until the latter half of the nineteenth century, when, as education advanced, the office gradually became extinct.

subjects affecting Hindus of the lower classes; while the "Andaroo" (*i.e.* Andhiyaru, a Parsi priest) was required in disputes and cases involving Parsis, whose customs in respect of marriage, divorce and inheritance had not at this date been codified and given the force of law.

The Regulation of 1812 effected little or no improvement in the state of the public security. Gangs of criminals burned ships in Bombay waters to defraud the insurance-companies; robberies by armed gangs occurred frequently in all parts of the Island;[1] and every householder of consequence was compelled to employ private watchmen, the fore-runners of the modern Ramosi and Bhaya, who were often in collusion with the bad characters of the more disreputable quarters of the Town.[2] Even Colaba, which contained few dwellings, was described in 1827 as the resort of thieves.[3] The executive head of the force at this date was Mr. Richard Goodwin, who succeeded the unfortunate Briscoe in 1811 and served until 1816, when apparently he was appointed Senior Magistrate of Police, with Mr. W. Erskine as his Junior.

The proceedings of both the magistrates and the police were regarded with a jaundiced eye by the Recorder's Court, and Sir Edward West, who filled the appointment, first of Recorder and then of Chief Justice, from 1822 to 1828, animadverted severely in 1825 upon the illegalities perpetrated by the magisterial courts, presided over at that date by Messrs. J. Snow and W. Erskine[4]. His successor in the Supreme Court,[5] Sir J. P. Grant, passed equally severe strictures upon the

One Samuel Nissim was Kazi in 1800 (Gazetteer of Bombay City & Island, Vol I, pp. 250 ff.)

1. One of the most notorious gangs was that of a certain Ali Paru, described in the *Times of India* of July 27, 1872.
2. *Bombay Courier*, March 3rd, 1827.
3. Gazetteer of Bombay City and Island, Vol. II, p. 143.
4. One Thomas Holloway appears in the Annual Register as "High Constable" in 1827.
5. The Supreme Court supplanted the Recorder's Court in 1823, and was opened in 1824.

police administration at the opening of the Quarter Sessions in 1828.

> "The calendar is a heavy one. Several of the crimes betoken a contempt of public justice almost incredible and a state of morals inconsistent with any degree of public prosperity. Criminals have not only escaped, but seem never to have been placed in jeopardy. The result is a general alarm among native inhabitants. We are told that you are living under the laws of England. The only answer is that it is impossible. What has been administered till within a few years back has not been the law of England, nor has it been administered in the spirit of the law of England; else it would have been felt in the ready and active support the people would have given to the law and its officers, and in the confidence people would have reposed in its efficacy for their protection."[1]

The punishments inflicted at this date were on the whole almost as barbarous as those in vogue in earlier days. In 1799, for example, we read of a Borah, Ismail Sheikh, being hanged for theft: in 1804 a woman was sentenced to five years' imprisonment for perjury, during which period she was to stand once a year, on the first day of the October Sessions, in the pillory in front of the Court House (afterwards the Great Western Hotel), with labels on her breast and back describing her crime: and in the same year one Harjivan was sentenced to be executed and hung in chains, presumably on Cross Island (*Chinal Tekri*), where the bodies of malefactors were usually exposed at this epoch. One James Pennico, who was convicted of theft in 1804, escaped lightly with three months' imprisonment and a public whipping at the cart's tail from Apollo Gate to Bazaar Gate; in 1806 a man who stole a watch was sentenced to two years' labour in the Bombay Docks.[2] The public pillory and flogging were punishments constantly inflicted during the early years of the nineteenth century.

1. F. D. Drewitt, *Bombay in the days of George IV*.
2. P. B. Malabari, *Bombay in the Making*, p. 283.

The pillory, which was in charge of the Deputy of Police, was located on the Esplanade in the neighbourhood of the site now occupied by the Municipal Offices. The last instance of its use occurred in 1834, when two Hindus were fastend in it by sentence of the Supreme Court and were pelted by boys for about an hour with a mixture composed of red earth, cowdung, decayed fruits and bad eggs. At intervals their faces were washed by two low-caste Hindus, and the pelting of filth was then resumed to the sound of a fanfaronade of horns blown by the Bhandaris attached to the Court.[1] Meanwhile the English doctrine of the equality of all men before the law was gradually being established, though the earliest instance of a Brahman being executed for a crime of violence did not occur until 1846. The case caused considerable excitement among orthodox Hindus, whose views were based wholly upon the laws of Manu.[2]

The early "thirties" were remarkable for much crime and for a serious public disturbance, the Parsi-Hindu riots, which broke out in July, 1832, in consequence of a Government order for the destruction of pariah-dogs, which at this date infested every part of the Island. Two European constables, stimulated by the reward of eight annas for every dog destroyed, were killing one in the proximity of a house, when they were attacked and severely handled by a mob composed of Parsis and Hindus of several sects. On the following day all the shops in the Town were closed, and a mob of about 300 roughs commenced to intimidate all persons who attempted to carry out their daily business. The bazar was deserted; and the mob forcibly destroyed the provisions intended for the Queen's Royals, who were on duty in the Castle, and stopped all supplies of food and water for the residents of Colaba and the shipping in the harbour. As the mob continued to gather strength, Mr. de Vitré, the Senior Magistrate of Police, called for

1. *Times of India*, September 22, 1894.
2. Gazetteer of Bombay City and Island, Vol. II, p. 224 (note 2.)

assistance from the garrison, which quickly quelled the disturbance.[1]

The Press of this date recorded constant cases of burglary and dacoity. "The utmost anxiety and alarm prevail amongst the inhabitants of this Island, especially those residing in Girgaum, Mazagon, Byculla and the neighbourhood, in consequence of the depredations and daring outrages committed by gangs of robbers armed with swords, pistols and even musquets, who, from the open and fearless manner in which they proceed along the streets, sometimes carrying torches with them, seem to dread neither opposition nor detection, and to defy the police." It was even said that sepoys of the 4th Regiment of Native Infantry, then stationed in the Island, joined these gangs of marauders, and when two men of the 11th Regiment were arrested on suspicion by a magistrate, their comrades stoned the magistrate's party. "It would be far better that the Island should be vacated altogether by the sepoy regiments," said the *Courier*, "than that it should be exposed repeatedly to these excesses." Fifty men of the Poona Auxiliary Force had to be brought down to aid the police and to patrol the roads at night.[2]

According to Mrs. Postans, the police administration had improved and robberies had become less frequent at the date of her visit, 1838. "The establishment of an efficient police force," she writes, "is one of the great modern improvements of the Presidency. Puggees (*Pagis i. e.* professional trackers) are still retained for the protection of property: but the highways and bazaars are now orderly and quiet, and robberies much less frequent."[3] The authoress admitted, however, that the Esplanade—particularly the portion of it occupied by the

1. Gazetteer of Bombay City and Island, Vol. II, p. 146-7.
2. S. T. Sheppard, *The Byculla Club*, p. 5.
3. Mrs. Postans, *Western India in 1838*, Vol. I, p. 27. The *Pagis* received about Rs. 7 a month for prowling about the compounds of houses by night.

tents of military cadets—was the resort of "a clique of dexterous plunderers," who during the night used to cast long hooks into the tents and so withdraw all the loose articles and personal effects within reach.[1] The prevalence of more serious crime is indicated by her remarks about the Bhandari toddy-drawers :—

> "It appears that in many cases of crime brought to the notice of the Bombay magistracy, evidence which has condemned the accused has been elicited from a Bundarrie, often sole witness of the culprit's guilt. Murderers, availing themselves of the last twilight ray to decoy their victims to the closest depths of the palmy woods and there robbing them of the few gold or silver ornaments they might possess, have little thought of the watchful toddy-drawer, in his lofty and shaded eyry."[2]

That the improvement was not very marked is also proved by the fact that in 1839, the year after Mrs. Postans' visit, the Bench of Justices increased their contribution to Government for police charges to Rs. 10,000, the additional cost being declared necessary owing to the rapid expansion of the occupied urban area, and to the grave inadequacy of the force for coping with crime. So far as watch and ward duties were concerned, the police must have welcomed the first lighting of the streets with oil-lamps in 1843. Ten years later there were said to be 50 lamps in existence, which were lighted from dusk to midnight, and the number continued to increase until October, 1865, when the first gas-lamps were lighted in the Esplanade and Bhendy Bazar. On the other hand drunkenness was a fruitful source of crime, and the number of country liquor-shops was practically unlimited. "On a moderate computation" wrote Mrs. Postans "every sixth shop advertises the sale of toddy." With such facilities for intoxication, crime was scarcely likely to decrease.

1. Ibid, Vol. II, p. 222.
2. Mrs. Postans, *Western India in 1838*, Vol. I, p. 92.

But other and deeper reasons existed for the unsatisfactory state of the public peace and security. Throughout the whole of the period from 1800 to 1850, and in a milder form till the establishment of the High Court in 1861, there was constant friction, occasionally of an acute character, between the Supreme Court and the Company's government and officials. Moreover, the original intention of the Crown that the Supreme Court should act as a salutary check upon the Company's administration was frustrated by several periods of interregnum between 1828 and 1855, the Court being represented frequently by only one Judge and on one occasion being entirely closed owing to the absence of judges. This antagonism between the highest judicial tribunal and the executive authority could not fail to react unfavourably on the subordinate machinery of the administration, and coupled with inadequacy of numbers, insufficiency of pay, and a general lack of integrity in the Police force itself, may be held to have been largely responsible for the comparative freedom enjoyed by wrong-doers and their manifest contempt for authority.

Contemporary records indicate that the Police Office at this period (1800-1850) was located in the Fort; the court of the Senior Magistrate of Police was housed in a building in Forbes Street, and the court of the Second Magistrate in a house in Mazagon. The powers of both Magistrates were limited, and all cases involving sentences of more than six months' imprisonment, or affecting property valued at more than Rs. 50, had to be sent to the Court of Petty Sessions or committed to the Recorder's, subsequently the Supreme Court. The Court of Petty Sessions was composed of the two Magistrates of Police and a Justice of the Peace (the Superintendent-General of Sir J. Mackintosh's draft Regulation), and sat every Monday morning at 10 a. m. at the Police Office in the Fort. The constitution of this Court was afterwards amended by Rule, Ordinance and Regulation I of 1834, which, though not registered in the

Supreme Court as required by Act XLVII, Geo. III, was subsequently legalized by India Act VII of 1836. By that Ordinance the Court was composed of not less than three Justices of the Peace, one of whom was a Magistrate of Police, the second was a European, and the third was a Native of India, not born of European parents. It remained in existence, with extended powers, until the year 1877, when, together with three Magistrates of Police, it was superseded by the Presidency Magistrates Act.

A word may here be said on the subject of the well-known uniform of the Bombay constabulary, the bright yellow cap and the dark blue tunic and knickers, which once caused a wag to style the Bombay police-sepoy "the empty black bottle with the yellow seal." The origin of the uniform is obscure; but it was certainly in use in 1838, for Mrs. Postans describes the dress of the men as "a dark blue coat, black belt, and yellow turban."[1] An illustration in *The Adventures of Qui-Hi,* entitled "A Night in Dongri," shows that the uniform was worn at a still earlier date. In the background of the picture two persons are obviously having an altercation with a police-constable, and the latter is depicted wearing the flat yellow cap and blue uniform familiar to every modern resident of Bombay. The dress of the constabulary must therefore have been adopted at some date prior to 1816, and it is probably a legitimate inference that it dates back to the reorganization of 1812, and was possibly adapted from an older dress worn at the end of the eighteenth century. In any case the distinctive features of the dress of the Bombay police-constable of to-day are well over one hundred years old.

When Thomas Holloway relinquished the office of High Constable in 1829, his place was taken by one José Antonio, presumably a Portuguese Eurasian, who had been serving as Constable to the Court of Petty

1. Mrs. Postans, *Western India in 1838,* Vol. I, p. 27.

Sessions. José Antonio seems to have performed the duties of executive police officer until 1835, when Captain Shortt was appointed "Superintendent of Police and Surveyor etc. etc". Between 1829 and 1855 the following officials were responsible for the police administration of Bombay :—

Period of Office	Senior Magistrate	Junior Magistrate	Constable or Supdt. of Police
1829–33	J. D. de Vitré	H. Gray	José Antonio
1834	J. Warden	Do.	Do.
			Supdt. of Police
1835–39	J. Warden	H. Willis	Capt. Shortt
1840	J. Warden	E. F. Danvers	Capt. Burrows
1841–45	P. W. Le Geyt	Do.	Do.
1846	G. L. Farrant	Do.	Capt. W. Curtis
1847–48	G. Grant	Do.	Do.
1849	Do.	Do.	Capt. E. Baynes
1850–51	A. Spens	Do.	Do.
1852–53	Do.	L. C. C. Rivett	Do.
1854–55	A. K. Corfield	T. Thornton	Do.

It will be apparent from this list that from 1835 to 1855 the executive control of the Police force was entrusted to a series of junior officers belonging to the Company's military forces, who probably possessed little or no aptitude for police work, were poorly paid for their services, and had no real encouragement to make their mark in civil employ. Consequently, despite increased expenditure on the force, these military Superintendents of Police secured very little control over the criminal classes, and effected no real improvement in the *morale* of their subordinates. In 1844, for example, a succession of daring robberies was carried out in the Harbour by gangs of criminals, who sailed round in boats from Back Bay. The most notorious of them was known as the Bandar Gang[1]; and their unchecked excesses led to the formation of a separate floating police-force under the control of a Deputy Superintendent on Rs. 500 a month. House-breaking was of daily occurrence in Colaba, Sonapur, Kalbadevi and Girgaum,[2] and constant complaints of dishonesty among the European constables and of the gross inefficiency of the native rank and file were made to the authorities by both public bodies and private residents.[3] Corruption was prevalent in all ranks of the force, and most of the subordinate officers, both European and Indian, were in secret collusion with agents and go-betweens, some of them members of the higher Hindu castes, who assisted their acts of extortion and blackmail and shared with them the proceeds of their venality. Bands of ruffians infested the thoroughfares and lanes of the native city, and no respectable resident dared venture unprotected into the streets after nightfall.

The period immediately preceding the year of the Mutiny was also remarkable for two serious breaches of the public peace. The earlier occurred at Mahim in 1850, on the last day of the Muharram festival, in consequence of a dispute between two factions of the Khoja community, and resulted in the murder of three men and the wounding of several others.[4] The later riots broke out in October, 1851, between the Parsis and Muhammadans, in consequence of a very indiscreet article on the Muhammadan religion which was published in the *Gujarati*, a Parsi newspaper. The Muhammadans, incensed at the statements made about the Prophet,

1. *Bombay Times*, Feb. 22, 1845.
2. Ibid., July 31, 1844.
3. Report of Bombay Chamber of Commerce, 1854-55, pp. 11, 12.
4. *Bombay Times*, December 14th, 1850.

gathered at the Jama Masjid on October 17th in very large numbers, and after disabling a small police patrol, stationed there to keep the peace, commenced attacking the Parsis and destroying their property. The public-conveyance stables at Paidhoni, which at that date belonged to Parsis, were wrecked, liquor-shops were broken open and rifled, shops and private houses were pillaged. Captain Baynes, the Superintendent of Police, and Mr. Spens, the Senior Magistrate, managed with a strong force to disperse the main body of rioters, capturing eighty-five of them: but towards evening, as there were signs of a fresh outbreak and the neighbourhood of Bhendy Bazaar was practically in a state of siege, the garrison-troops were marched down to Mumbadevi and thence distributed in pickets throughout the area of disturbance. This action finally quelled the rioting, and the annual Muharram festival, which commenced ten days later, passed off without any untoward incident.[1]

In the year 1855 the post of Senior Magistrate was held by Mr. Corfield, Messrs. T. Thornton and N. W. Oliver being respectively Junior and Third Magistrates. In that year the public outcry against the police had become so great, and the general insecurity had been reflected in so constant a series of crimes against person and property, that Lord Elphinstone's government determined to institute a searching enquiry into the whole subject. With this object they appointed to the immediate command of the force in 1856 Mr. Charles Forjett, who was serving at the moment as Deputy Superintendent. Through his energy and activity, they were able to satisfy themselves fully of the prevalence of wholesale corruption in the force. Drastic executive action was at once taken; and this was followed by the drafting and promulgation of Act XIII of 1856 for the future constitution and regulation of the Police Force. At the same time Mr. Corfield was succeeded as Senior Magistrate by Mr. W. Crawford. The credit for the

1. *Bombay Times*, October 18, 1851.

introduction of the reforms and for the restoration of public confidence belongs wholly to Charles Forjett, whose successful administration during a period fraught with grave political dangers deserves to be recorded in a separate chapter. His appointment in 1855 may be said to inaugurate the *régime* of the professional police official as distinguished from the purely military officer, and to mark the final disappearance of an antiquated system, under which inefficiency and crime flourished exceedingly. Henceforth a new standard of administration was imposed, whereby the Bombay Police Force was enabled to maintain the public peace effectively and also to acquire by degrees a larger share of the confidence and co-operation of the general body of citizens.[1]

1. *Report on the Administration of Public Affairs in the Bombay Presidency for 1855-56.* "During the year 1855 great reforms have been effected in the Police within the jurisdiction of His Majesty's Supreme Court. Complaints were made by the Chamber of Commerce of the venality of the European constables and of the inefficiency of the general force. These complaints, and other circumstnces which induced suspicion, determined Government to place in immediate command of the Police, Mr. Forjett, the most active and efficient of the Mofussil Superintendents, a gentleman who had once been a Foujdar, and who had risen to high and responsible appointments, solely through his own remarkable energy, acuteness and ability. An enquiry by this gentleman soon showed the existence of corruption among the European Constables, a corruption which impaired the efficiency of the whole force. A considerable number were summarily dismissed, and a thorough reform in Police arrangements throughout the Island was commenced by the new Superintendent. These are still in progress: but the Government has been assured that a feeling of entire security as to life and property is now entertained by all classes of the community."

CHAPTER III

Mr. Charles Forjett
1855-1863

Charles Forjett[1], who was appointed Superintendent of Police in 1855, was of Eurasian (now styled Anglo-Indian) parentage and was brought up in India. His father was an officer of the old Madras Fort Artillery and had been wounded at the capture of Seringapatam in 1799. In *Our Real Danger in India*, which he published in 1877, some few years after his retirement, Forjett states that he served the Bombay Government for forty years, first as a topographical surveyor and then successively as official translator in Marathi and Hindustani, Sheriff, head of the Poona police, subordinate and chief uncovenanted assistant judge, superintendent of police in the Southern Maratha Country, and finally as Commissioner of Police, Bombay. He first earned the favourable notice of the Bombay Government by his reform and reorganization of the police in the Belgaum division of the Southern Maratha Country; and there is probably considerable justification for his own statement that the peace and security of the southern districts of the Presidency during the period of the Mutiny were chiefly due to his constructive work in this direction.

He owed his later success as a police-officer to three main factors, namely his great linguistic faculty, his wide knowledge of Indian caste-customs and habits, and his masterly capacity for assuming native disguises. Born

1. Mr. B. Aitken in *Old and New Bombay* states that Forjett was partly of French descent, and that the family name was originally Forget. Owing to constant mispronunciation, Forjett eventually anglicised the name in the form now familiar to students of Bombay history.

and bred in India, he had learnt the vernaculars of the Bombay Presidency in his youth, and had been familiar from his earliest years with those subtle differences of belief and custom which the average home-bred Englishman knows nothing about and can never master. His black hair and sallow complexion—in brief, the strong "strain of the country" in his blood—enabled him, when disguised, to pass among natives of India as one of themselves. A story is told to illustrate his powers of disguise. He once told the Governor, Lord Elphinstone, that in spite of special orders prohibiting the entrance of any one and in defiance of the strongest military cordon that His Excellency could muster, he would effect his entrance to Government House, Parel, and appear at the Governor's bedside at 6 a. m.. Lord Elphinstone challenged him to fulfil his boast and took every precaution to prevent his ingress. Nevertheless Forjett duly appeared the following morning in the Governor's bedroom—in the disguise of a *mehtar* (sweeper). With these special qualifications for police work were combined a strong will and great personal courage.

Forjett's fame rests mainly upon his action during the Mutiny, and one is apt to overlook the great but less sensational services which he rendered to Government and the public in subduing lawlessness and crime in Bombay. As mentioned in the previous chapter, he was serving as Assistant or Deputy Superintendent of Police for some few months before Lord Elphinstone placed him in control of the force, and during that period he set himself to test the extent of the corruption which was believed to prevail widely among all ranks. By means of his disguises he managed to get into close touch with the men who were acting as go-betweens and receivers of bribes, and even dined with one of them, a high-caste Hindu, without betraying his identity. Through these men he also contrived on various occasions to test the integrity of individual members of the force. In consequence he was able in a very short time to expose the whole system of corruption and to furnish Government with the evidence they required for a drastic purging of the upper and lower grades.

That duty accomplished, he turned his attention to the criminal classes.[1] "At a time" wrote the late Mr. K. N. Kabraji in his *Reminiscences of Fifty Years Ago*, "when the public safety was quite insecure, when the city was infested by desperate gangs of thieves and other malefactors, Forjett had to use all his wonderful energy and acumen to break their power and rid the city of their presence. He strengthened and reformed the Police, which had been powerless to cope with them. There was a notorious band of athletic ruffians in Bazar Gate Street, consisting chiefly of Parsis. They used to occupy some rising ground, from which they swooped down on their prey. Their daily acts of crime and violence were committed with impunity, and their names were whispered by mothers to hush their children to silence.

"I may here give a personal instance of the insecurity of the times. As I was returning one night with my father from the Grant Road theatre in a carriage, a ruffian prowling about in the dark at Falkland road snatched my gold-embroidered cap and ran away with it. The road had been newly built and ran through fields and waste land. Khetwadi, as its name implies, was also an agricultural district. Grant road, Falkland road and Khetwadi were then lonely places on the outskirts of the City, and it is no wonder that wayfarers in these localities could never be secure of purse or person. But on the Esplanade, under the very walls of the Fort, occurred instances of violence and highway robbery, which went practically unchecked. Not a few of the offenders were soldiers. They used to lie in wait for a likely carriage with a rope thrown across the road, so that the horse stumbled and fell, and then they rifled the occupants of the carriage at

1. See General Adm. Report, Bombay, 1855-56 and 1858-59.

their leisure. It was Mr. Forjett, whose vigilance and activity brought all this crying scandal to an end."[1]

The rapid change for the better which followed Forjett's appointment to the office of Superintendent is illustrated by the fact that whereas in 1855 only 23 per cent of property stolen was recovered, in 1856 the percentage had risen to 59. Mr. W. Crawford, "Senior Magistrate of Police and Commissioner of Police", in his annual return of crime for the year 1859 remarked that "the total continued absence of gang and highway robbery is most satisfactory", and drew pointed attention to the efficiency of the "executive branch of the police" under Mr. Forjett.[2] In the following year, 1860, there were only three cases of burglary, and although the value of property stolen amounted to Rs. 187,000, the police managed to recover property worth Rs. 73,000. Serious offences against the person also seem to have decreased in number during Forjett's *régime*. The Senior Magistrate observed with satisfaction that "the debasing spectacle of a public execution was not called for" during the year 1859; and such records as still exist of the later years of Forjett's administration point to the same conclusion.[3]

It must not be assumed, however, that this period lacked *causes célèbres*. A brief reference to a few of the more important cases will serve to show the varied character of the enquiries carried out by the Police. In 1860 a European seaman, the chief mate of the *Lady Canning*, was arraigned before the Supreme Court for an attempt to administer poison to the Master and three others belonging to the vessel. The chief witness for the prosecution, however, though bound by recognizances

1. Gazetteer of Bombay City and Island, Vol. II, p. 244.
2. The Annual Adm. Rep. Bombay Pres. for 1858–59 mentions that only one case of burglary had occurred in that year and that "robberies with violence have entirely disappeared".
3. Annual Police Returns, showing state of crime, for 1859–61. (India Office Records).

to appear at the trial, sailed from Bombay before the proceedings commenced and could not be brought back. The prisoner was therefore acquitted. In the same year a Bene-Israel and two Hindus were convicted of piracy at the Sessions and sentenced to seven years' transportation, for having plundered a vessel at anchor off Alibag of ten thousand rupees in silver. In 1861 a Parsi contractor was committed for trial on a charge of manslaughter. He was in charge of the work of digging foundations for a new cotton-spinning mill in Tardeo (probably one of Sir Dinshaw Petit's mills), when an accident occurred in which five men lost their lives. The contractor was held to have shown a culpable lack of caution; but the Grand Jury threw out the bill against him, and further action was abandoned. A more famous case in the same year was the Bhattia Conspiracy Trial, connected with the famous Maharaja Libel Case of 1862, in which Gokuldas Liladhar and eight other Bhattias were accused of conspiracy to obstruct and defeat the course of justice, by intimidating witnesses and preventing them from giving evidence in the libel-suit brought by Jadunathji Brijratanji Maharaj against Karsondas Mulji and Nanabhai Ranina, editor and printer respectively of the *Satya Prakash*.[1] Forjett and one of his European constables, George Gahagan, gave evidence before the Supreme Court of the meeting of the conspirators. The accused were found guilty, and Sir Joseph Arnould sentenced the two leading members of the conspiracy to a fine of Rs. 1000 apiece, and the rest to a fine of Rs. 500 each. There was considerable disturbance in Court when these sentences were pronounced.

Forjett served as Superintendent of Police until the end of 1863 or the early part of 1864, with a period of leave to Europe in 1860, during which his work was carried on by Mr. Dunlop, Deputy Superintendent in

1. Report of the Maharaja Libel Case, Bombay Gazette Press, 1862.

charge of the Harbour or Water Police.[1] In addition to his duties as head of "the executive police," he was a member of the old Board of Conservancy (1845–1858), and later one of the triumvirate of Municipal Commissioners, established by Act XXV of 1858, which was responsible for the entire conservancy and improvement of the town of Bombay until its supersession in 1865 by a full-time Municipal Commissioner and the body corporate of the Justices. It was in this capacity that Forjett in 1863 conceived and inaugurated the project of converting the old dirty and dusty Cotton Green into what later generations know as the Elphinstone Circle. The scheme was warmly supported in turn by Lord Elphinstone and Sir Bartle Frere. The Municipal Commissioners bought up the whole site and resold it at a considerable profit in building-lots to English business firms; and by the end of 1865, two years after Forjett had proposed the scheme, the Elphinstone Circle was practically completed and ready for occupation.[2]

In addition to regular police duties, the Superintendent of Police at this date was also in charge of the Fire Brigade—an arrangement which lasted until 1888, and which accounts for the fact that an annual return of fires signed by Forjett and his successor formed a regular feature of the annual crime return submitted to Government by the Senior Magistrate of Police. The officers and men of the brigade were members of the regular police force, the European officers performing both police and fire-brigade duties and the Indian ranks being restricted to fire-duty only.[3]

1. Dunlop had been 3rd Assistant to the Master Attendant of the Government Dockyard, and was appointed head of the Water Police in 1844. Prior to that year no proper water police force was in existence.
2. Gazetteer of Bombay City and Island, Vol. III, 252; *Times of India*, January 2nd, 1865; Annual Adm. Rep. Bombay Presidency, 1862–63.
3. Gazetteer of Bombay City and Island, Vol. III, 49.

During Mr. Forjett's tenure of office, the post of Senior Magistrate was held by Mr. W. Crawford, between whom and the Superintendent of Police the most amicable relations existed. The position of both officials was considerably strengthened by the passing of Act XLVIII of 1860, amending Act XIII of 1856, which gave the police wider powers for the regulation and prevention of nuisances, and enabled the magistracy to deal promptly and effectively with offences to which the old Act of 1856 did not extend.[1]

The period of the Mutiny (1857) was fraught with anxiety for the English residents of Bombay. Between May and September rumours and hints of the probability of a rising of the native population were constantly disseminated, and more than one Indian of standing narrowly escaped arrest for treason as the result of false complaints laid before the authorities by interested parties. Among those thus secretly impeached was the famous millionaire, Mr. Jagannath Shankarshet (1804–65), who might well have succumbed to the attacks of his accusers, had the Governor, Lord Elphinstone, been less calm, circumspect and resolute. Jagannath's guilt was firmly believed in by several influential Englishmen, who brought their views to the notice of the Governor. He instructed Forjett to investigate the matter; and the latter was able to prove that the charges were wholly without foundation.[2] The belief in Jagannath's treasonable dealings with the mutineers in Bengal may perhaps have resulted from action taken by Forjett immediately after the outbreak of the Mutiny. In the garden of Jagannath Shankarshet's mansion was a large rest-house or *dharamshala* intended for the accommodation of wandering Brahman mendicants, who during the day begged food and alms in the town. *Sanyasis* and *Bhikshuks* from all parts of India visited this rest-house, bringing

1. Annual Crime Return, 1860; Gazetteer of Bombay City and Island, Vol. II, 244.
2. Gazetteer of Bombay City and Island, Vol. II, p. 157.

all kinds of information of events in Bengal and the upper Provinces: and Forjett lost no time in placing an intelligent up-country Brahman, disguised as a mendicant, on detective duty in the *dharamshala.* It is quite possible that this plan may have been partly responsible for the rumour that Jagannath was in collusion with the infamous Nana Saheb. On the other hand the detective must have supplied Forjett with much of the evidence which enabled him to disprove the Hindu millionaire's complicity in the Sepoy rebellion.[1]

At this date the military forces in Bombay comprised three native regiments and one British force of 400 men under the command of Brigadier Shortt. The native troops were implicitly trusted by their officers, and the chief danger apprehended by the Bombay Government was from the Muhammadan population of the city, which numbered about 150,000. Forjett from the first combated this view and wrote a special letter to the Governor's Private Secretary, warning him that the main danger was from the troops. His own inquiries had convinced him that the townspeople would not rise unless the native regiments gave them the lead, and that the latter were planning mutiny. Much to the disgust of General Shortt, he made no secret of his views, declaring that the sepoys were the real potential source of disturbance and danger. Forjett's own force consisted of 60 European police and a number of Indian constables; but on the fidelity of the latter he could not implicitly rely. Consequently, after news reached Bombay of the disasters at Cawnpore and other centres, he obtained Lord Elphinstone's special permission to enrol a body of 50 European mounted police.[2]

Meanwhile the Muharram, which was always an occasion of anxiety and frequently of disturbance, was

1. C. Forjett, *Our Real Danger in India*, 1877; *Bombay Gazette*, December 25th, 1907.
2. C. Forjett, *Our Real Danger in India*, 1877; Holmes, *History of the Indian Mutiny.*

drawing near. The plans made by the Government for maintaining order involved the division of the European troops and police into small parties, which were posted in various parts of the town.[1] Forjett disapproved wholly of this arrangement, as no considerable body of European troops or police would be at hand to quell a mutiny of the sepoys, which was certain to break out in the neighbourhood of their barracks. He was naturally not empowered to revise the arrangement of the military forces; but he definitely informed Lord Elphinstone that he felt bound to disobey the orders for the distribution of the police. "It is a very risky thing", said the Governor, "to disobey orders; but I am sure you will do nothing rash."[2]

Despite the risk, Forjett disobeyed the orders and concentrated all his efforts on outwitting the plotters. He summoned a meeting of the leading Muhammadans and addressed them in very strong terms on the subject of fomenting disorder—a step which earned Lord Elphinstone's personal commendation. Then, night after night, both before and during the celebration of the festival, he wandered about the city in disguise, and whenever he heard anyone speaking of the mutineers' successes in other parts of India in anything like a tone of exultation, he arrested him on the spot. A whistle brought up three or more of his detective police, who took charge of the culprit and marched him off to the lock-up. The bad characters of the town were so much alarmed by these mysterious arrests, which seemed to indicate that the authorities knew all that was afoot, that they relinquished their plans for an outbreak. In his dealings with the *badmash* element, Forjett received valuable assistance from the Kazi of

1. Apparently it was customary during the Muharram festival in the 'fifties of last century to post a body of 200 Europeans in "the Bhendy Bazar stables". Presumably additional European police were brought in from Poona and other districts. The Muharram danger was finally eradicated in 1912.
2. The Gazetteer of Bombay City and Island, Vol. II, 158.

Bombay, from a Muhammadan Subehdar of police, and from an Arab with whom he used, when disguised, to visit mosques, coffee-shops, and other places of popular resort.[1]

The Muharram would have ended peacefully but for the stupidity of a drunken Christian drummer, belonging to one of the native regiments, who towards the end of the festival insulted a religious procession of Hindus by knocking down the idol which they were escorting. He was at once arrested and locked up. The men of his regiment, incensed at the action of the police, whom they detested on account of Forjett's known distrust of themselves, hurried to the lock-up, released the drummer and carried him off, together with two police-guards, to their lines. An English constable and four Indian police-sepoys, who went to demand the surrender of the drummer and the release of their two comrades, were resisted by force. A struggle ensued, and the police had to fight their way out, leaving two of their number seriously wounded. The excitement was intense, and the sepoys of the native regiments were bent upon breaking out of their lines. On receiving news of the disturbance, Forjett galloped to the scene, leaving orders for his assistant, Mr. Edginton, and the European police to follow him. He found the native troops trying to force their way out of the lines, and their officers with drawn swords endeavouring to hold them back. At the sight of Forjett the anger of the men rose to white heat. "For God's sake Mr. Forjett," cried the officers, "go away". "If your men are bent on mischief" was the reply, "the sooner it is over the better." The sepoys hesitated, while Forjett sat on his horse confronting them. A minute or two later Mr. Edginton and fifty-four European police rode up; and Forjett cried, "Throw open the gates. I am ready for them." The native troops were unprepared for this prompt action, and judging discretion to be the better part of valour, remained in their lines and gradually recovered their senses.[2]

1. C. Forjett, *Our Real Danger in India*, 1877.
2. Gazetteer of Bombay City and Island, Vol. II, 158-9.

But the trouble, though scotched, was not killed. A few days later Forjett erected a gibbet in the compound of the Police Office, summoned the chief citizens whom he knew to be disaffected, and, pointing to the gibbet, warned them that on the slightest sign that they meditated an outbreak, they would be seized and hanged. This forcible demonstration had the desired effect. Forjett had quashed all chance of a rising in the bazar. But the danger from the native troops remained. Forjett redoubled his detective activities and soon discovered that a number of them were regularly holding secret meetings in the house of one Ganga Prasad, who had gained the confidence of the sepoys in the triple rôle of priest, devotee and physician.[1] Forjett had this man arrested and induced him to confess all he knew. The next night he went in disguise to the house in Sonapur (Dhobi Talao) and listened to the sepoys' conversation. He learnt that they intended to mutiny during the Hindu festival of Divali in October, pillage the city, and then escape from the Island. He reported the facts at once to the military officers, who received them with incredulity. But Forjett eventually persuaded Major Barrow, the commandant of one of the regiments, to accompany him in disguise to the house and hear the details of the plot from a convenient hiding-place. Major Barrow was convinced and reported the facts to General Shortt, who exclaimed :—"Mr. Forjett has caught us at last ! " Court-martials were promptly held : the two ringleaders—a native officer of the Marine Battalion and a private of the 10th N. I.—were blown from guns on the Esplanade, and six of their accomplices were transported for life. According to James Douglas, thirty men deserved the same fate as the ringleaders, but owed their reprieve to the clemency of Lord Elphinstone.[2]

Thus by his energy, courage and detective ability did Forjett save Bombay from a mutiny of the garrison.

1. C. Forjett, *Our Real Danger in India.*

2. Douglas, *Bombay and W. India*, I, 211.

His services had more than local effect, for in Lord Elphinstone's opinion, if the Mutiny in Bombay had been successful, nothing could have saved Hyderabad, Poona and the rest of the Presidency, and after that "Madras was sure to go too."[1] The formal thanks of the Bombay Government were conveyed to Forjett in a letter from the Secretary, Judicial Department, No. 1681 of May 23rd, 1859, nearly six months after the Queen's Proclamation announcing the end of the East India Company's rule. The words of the letter were as follows:—

"The Right Honourable the Governor in Council avails himself of this opportunity of expressing his sense of the very valuable services rendered by the Deputy Commissioner of Police,[2] Mr. Forjett, in the detection of the plot in Bombay in the autumn of 1857. His duties demanded great courage, great acuteness, and great judgment, all of which qualities were conspicuously displayed by Mr. Forjett at that trying period."

The scars left by the Mutiny in India were barely healed, when Bombay entered upon that extraordinary era of prosperity, engendered by the outbreak of the American Civil war and the consequent stoppage of the American cotton-supply, which gave her in five years 81 millions sterling more than she had regarded in previous years as a fair price for her cotton, and which eventually led, after a period of great inflation, to the financial disasters of 1865. An enormous influx of population took place; the occupied area rapidly expanded; and the

1. C. Forjett, *Our Real Danger in India.*
2. The use of the phrase "Deputy Commissioner of Police" is explained by the fact that, strictly speaking, the Senior Magistrate was at this date Commissioner of Police, and Forjett as head of the "executive police" was his Deputy. Forjett in his book speaks of himself as Commissioner of Police: but this title was not given to the head of the force till 1865 In the Senior Magistrate's Annual Crime Return for 1860 Forjett is styled Superintendent of Police: but in his evidence before the Supreme Court in the Bhattia Conspiracy Case, Forjett stated, "In my official capacity as Deputy Commissioner of Police, I received a letter."

burden thrown upon the police force, which was numerically inadequate, must have been excessive. It redounds to Forjett's credit that in spite of all difficulties, and in conjunction with his duties as a Municipal Commissioner in a time of feverish urban progress, he contrived to keep crime within reasonable bounds, and put an end finally to the hordes of ruffians who infested the skirts of the town and nightly lay in wait for passers-by.[1]

The Indian merchants of Bombay were not slow to recognise his services to the city, and showed their gratitude for the security which he had afforded to them by presenting him in 1859 with an address, and subscribing at the same time "a sum of upwards of £1300 sterling for the purpose of offering to him a more enduring token of their esteem."[2] That was not all. After his retirement to England early in 1864, the Indian cotton-merchants sent him a purse of £1500, "in token of their strong gratitude for one whose almost despotic powers and zealous energy had so quelled the explosive forces of native society that they seem to have become permanently subdued:" while the Back Bay Reclamation Company, which was formed at the height of the share mania, allotted him five shares in his absence, and when the price reached a high point, sold them and sent him the proceeds in the form of a draft for £13,580.[3] These large sums, presented to Forjett after his final departure from India, form a striking testimony to the value of his work as a police-officer and to the great impression left by his personality upon Indians of all classes in Bombay.

Forjett's services at the time of the Mutiny were separately acknowledged. From the public he received various addresses and a purse of £3,850, subscribed by

1. In earlier days one of the chief haunts of these gangs was a deep hollow near the site of the present Arthur Crawford Market (J. M. Maclean, *Guide to Bombay*, 1902, p. 206.)
2. Gazetteer of Bombay City and Island, II, 244; Ann. Adm. Rep. Bombay Presidency, 1858—59.
3. C. Forjett, *Our Real Danger in India*.

both English and Indian residents. The Government, whose eulogy of his action has already been quoted, granted him an extra pension and also bestowed a commission in the Army upon his son, F. H. Forjett, who was in command of one of the native regiments in Bombay at the time of the great Hindu-Muhammadan riots of 1893.[1] Yet Forjett is said to have regarded himself as slighted by Government in not having received from them any decoration.[2] It certainly seems curious that so admirable a public servant should not have been rewarded with a Knighthood or admitted to one of the Orders of Chivalry. But in Forjett's day the Government bestowed decorations very sparingly, and it may have been thought that this faithful servant of the vanished East India Company was sufficiently recompensed by the grant of a commission to his son and by permission to accept the handsome pecuniary rewards offered to him by a grateful urban population.

After his retirement, Forjett purchased a property near Hughenden, which he called "Cowasjee Jehangir Hall" after the well-known Parsi philanthropist, who gave so largely to educational and charitable institutions in Western India.[3] In 1877 he published *Our Real Danger in India*, in which he sought to explain the lesson of his own experience during the Mutiny and gave an account of the events of that period in Bombay. He died in London on January 27th 1890, but at what age is unknown, as the date of his birth has never been satisfactorily determined. He can hardly have been less

1. F. H. Forjett joined the 59th Foot in 1865 and in 1870 was transferred to the Bombay Staff Corps. He served mostly in the 26th Bombay N. I., which in the "seventies" and "eighties" was known familiarly as the "Black Watch", owing to its having no less than three Eurasian British officers, namely John Miles, the Commandant, a half-caste of dominating personality, John M. Heath and F. H. Forjett.
2. C. E. Buckland, *Dictionary of Indian Biography.*
3. J. Douglas, *Bombay and Western India*, I, 211.

than thirty-five years of age when he was appointed Superintendent of the Bombay Police in 1855, and was possibly older. Sir Lees Knowles of Westwood, Pendlebury, met him in 1886, and describes him at that date as "a man of middle height, with a very pale olive complexion, and highly nervous: he could not without shaking raise a glass of water to his lips."[1] Forjett's pension was paid in rupees, and after the more or less permanent decline in the exchange-value of the rupee, he requested the British Government on more than one occasion to permit him to draw his pension in sterling, but failed to obtain sanction to his request.

Here it is well to take leave of Charles Forjett, the first efficient chief that the Bombay Police ever had. One hesitates to imagine what might have happened in Bombay, if a man of less courage and ability had been in charge of the force in 1857: and looking back upon all that he achieved during his nine years of office, one realizes why Lord Elphinstone trusted him so implicitly, and why the Indian and European public regarded him with so much respect and admiration. His name still lives in Forjett Street, a thoroughfare of minor importance leading from Cumballa hill into the mill-area of Tardeo. He himself will live for ever in the history of the "First City in India" as the man who raised the whole tone of police administration, brought the criminal classes of Bombay for the first time under stern control, and saved the city from the horrors and excesses which must inevitably have attended a rebellion of the native garrison.

1. Letter to *Morning Post*, August 30th, 1921.

CHAPTER IV

SIR FRANK SOUTER KT., C.S.I.
1864—1888

Forjett was succeeded in 1864 by Mr. Frank H. Souter, son of Captain Souter of the 44th Regiment who was a prisoner in Afghanistan in 1842. Mr. Souter had served as a volunteer against the rebels in the Nizam's dominions in 1850, and was appointed Superintendent of Police, Dharwar, in 1854. During the Mutiny he captured the rebel chief of Nargund, for which he received a sword of honour, and two years later (1859) was engaged in suppressing the Bhil brigands of the northern Deccan. This task he successfully completed by killing Bhagoji Naik, the notorious Bhil outlaw, and capturing his chief followers, showing on several occasions so much courage and resource that he was recommended for the Victoria Cross. He thus had several years of distinguished service to his credit before he assumed charge of the Bombay Police Force in 1864.

The appointment of Mr. Souter, who was awarded the C. S. I. in 1868 and was knighted by H. R. H. the Prince of Wales in 1875, synchronized with a thorough revision of the strength of the force. As already stated, the period 1860-65 witnessed a phenomenal expansion of the town, in consequence of the great profits derived from the sale of cotton during the American Civil War. Much reclamation of land from the sea was carried out, the mill-industry throve apace, the town spread northward with amazing rapidity, and shoals of immigrants of all classes poured into Bombay in the hope of making a fortune or securing a livelihood from the many economic and industrial projects then floated. In the large army of workers that invaded the Island there

SIR FRANK SOUTER

were naturally many persons of bad character and shady antecedents, who soon found their level among the criminal classes and helped to swell the crime-returns. It was obvious at the date of Mr. Forjett's retirement that the police-force had not been augmented *pari passu* with the growth of the population and the expansion of the residential area, and the Census of 1864, carried out by the Health Officer under the instruction of Sir Bartle Frere's government, proved beyond cavil that the force was quite inadequate to deal with the population of 816,562 then recorded.

Accordingly in 1864 Colonel Bruce, Inspector-General of Police with the Government of India, was despatched to Bombay to investigate local conditions and make recommendations for the future constitution of the force. His proposals, which were approved and adopted in 1865, were briefly the following. The total force was to number 1456, as he was "unable to perceive that the work could be done with fewer hands", divided under the following main heads:—

Land Police	1239
Police Guards for Government buildings	116
Harbour Police	101
Total ...	1456

Besides these, there were 84 police for the Government Dockyard, who had existed for several years and were paid for by the Marine Department, and a few miscellaneous police, who guarded municipal graveyards and burning-grounds and were paid for by the Municipal Commissioners. Neither these nor the Dock police were available for ordinary police work. Excluding the Harbour police, who numbered 101, the police force proper in 1865 was composed as follows :—

Superintendents	6
Inspectors	22
Sub-Inspectors	12

Jemadars	24
Havildars	62
Men	1216
Mounted Police	13[1]

These numbers were appreciably in excess of the total strength of the force in Mr. Forjett's time and placed the Bombay police on a level with the forces maintained in the sister-towns of Calcutta and Madras.

The office of Commissioner of Police dates also from Colonel Bruce's reorganization of 1865. He proposed that the appointments of Police Commissioner and Municipal Commissioner should be amalgamated: but this suggestion was very wisely negatived by Government. The senior officer of the police force was thenceforth made responsible solely for the police administration of the city, with the title of Police Commissioner, while under the new Municipal Act of 1865 the executive power and responsibility in municipal matters were vested in a Municipal Commissioner, appointed for a term of three years. From this date, therefore, the Commissioner of Police, though he still controlled the fire-brigade and sat on the Municipal Corporation as an elected or nominated member, ceased to exercise any official powers in regard to conservancy, rating, lighting and the water-supply.

For the first thirteen years of Sir Frank Souter's tenure of office, the old system of Magistrates of Police and the Court of Petty Sessions continued unaltered. In 1866, for example, when Sir F. Souter took furlough and Major Henderson was acting for him, the Senior Magistrate was Mr. J. P. Bickersteth, with Messrs. F. L. Brown and Dosabhai Framji Karaka as his colleagues. He was succeeded in turn by Mr. Barton, Mr. John Connon, in whose memory the John Connon High School was founded, and Mr. C. P. Cooper, who was in substantive

1. Prior to 1865 there appear to have been 26 mounted police.
2. First Annual Rep. of the Commissioner of Police, 1884; Gazetteer of Bombay City and Island, II, 245.

charge of the office at the time of the passing of the Presidency Magistrates Act IV of 1877. This Act abolished the Magistrates of Police and the Court of Petty Sessions, and invested the Presidency Magistrates, who succeeded them, with powers to deal with all cases formerly committed to the Petty Sessions, and with a large number of cases formerly triable only by the High Court. Nevertheless the Chief Presidency Magistrate continued for a few years longer to submit an annual report to Government on the state of crime in Bombay, which contained *inter alia* a few returns, and occasionally a few remarks on undetected murder cases, by the Commissioner of Police.

These annual reports of the Senior Magistrate, and later the Chief Presidency Magistrate, were doleful documents, consisting of a mass of figures relative to various classes of crime, and unrelieved, except on very rare occasions, by illuminating comment or interesting fact. The reviews by Government of these returns were little better. Occasionally an Under-Secretary would try to infuse life into the dry bones of the crime-tables, and suggest new avenues of inquiry : but in the end the figures, like the thorns of Holy Writ, sprang up and choked him, and he had to content himself with echoing the uninspired deductions of the magisterial bench. In 1883 the Bombay Government decreed the abolition of these magisterial reports on the state of crime, and in the following year Sir Frank Souter, as Commissioner of Police, submitted the first annual report on the working of the Police in the Town and Island of Bombay. The change, though overdue, was none the less welcome, for the Commissioner, with his fingers on the pulse of the city, was in a position to supply more valuable information and lend a more human touch to the report than was possible so long as his annual review of police activity was confined to a list of fires and a table showing dismissals and resignations from the force. The Chief

1. G. R. J. D. No. 5628 of August 10th, 1883.

Presidency Magistrate, with a tenacity worthy of a better cause, continued to submit a return of crime until 1886, when Government ordered its discontinuance. Since that date the only annual report on police and crime has been furnished by the Commissioner, who is accustomed to forward it for remarks to the Chief Presidency Magistrate before submitting it to Government.

During the later years of Sir Frank Souter's *régime* the police force was seriously undermanned. Colonel Bruce's proposals had brought it to approximately the right strength in 1865, but the city continued to expand so rapidly that the numbers then deemed adequate no longer sufficed for the purposes of watch and ward. In 1871 the force numbered 1473, of whom 285 were paid by Government and 1188 by the Municipality, exclusive of 396 men who did duty on the railways. In the following year the Senior Magistrate of Police, John Connon, remarked that "the European Police Force, though now too much reduced, is upon the whole a most respectable body of men, always ready for duty and capable of it. I can conscientiously say as much of numbers of natives of different ranks in the force."[1] The reduction in numbers, to which he referred, apparently lasted for several years, the total strength of the force varying from 1402 in 1873 to 1408 in 1877. In 1879 it had decreased still further to 1392 men, of whom 262 were classed as Government and 1130 as municipal police (*i. e.* paid by the Municipal Corporation). In 1881 the number paid for by Government had risen to 324, but the number of "municipal police" was less by 58 than in 1871. The subject was alluded to by the Commissioner in his annual report of June 6th, 1885, and he emphasized the fact that, despite minor increases during the previous twenty years and in spite of a definite expansion of the scope and character of police-work, he was actually in command of 101 men less than in 1865.

1. Annual Crime Return, 1872.

In 1885 the Bombay Police Force was composed as follows :—

(*a*) *Land Police*

- 1 Commissioner of Police
- 1 Deputy Commissioner of Police
- 6 Superintendents
- 36 Officers on Rs. 100 per month and over
- 92 Officers on less than Rs. 100 per month
- 1020 Constables

(*b*) 98 Police guards for Government buildings

(*c*) *Harbour Police*

- 1 Superintendent
- 13 Subordinate Officers
- 87 Constables

(*d*) *Dockyard Police*

- 7 Subordinate Officers
- 77 Constables

(*e*) 5 Police-guards for distilleries

(*f*) *C. D. Act Police*

- 2 Subordinate Officers
- 10 Constables

(*g*) *Prince's Dock Police*

- 6 Subordinate Officers
- 44 Constables

(*h*) 20 Constables at burning and burial grounds.

The total cost of this force, including rent, contingencies, allowances and hospital expenses, was Rs. 475,297. The cost of the Land Police was borne by Government, the Municipal Corporation giving a fixed contribution towards it. The Corporation paid also for the constables posted at the burning and burial grounds. Government bore the whole cost of the Harbour Police, while the charges of the Prince's Dock Police were debited to the Port Trustees.

While the force numbered 101 less than in 1865, the population of Bombay had increased from 645,000 in 1872 to 773,000 in 1881; while between 1872 and 1883 nearly 4000 new dwelling-houses had been erected and 6½ miles of new streets and roads had been thrown open to traffic. Again, whereas in Calcutta the percentage of police to population was 1 to 227, in Bombay the percentage was 1 to 506. In consequence the strain upon the men was excessive. Most of them worked both by day and night and obtained no proper rest: and this fact, coupled with the exiguous pay of Rs. 10 per month allotted to the lowest grade constable, injured recruitment and obliged the Commissioner to accept candidates of less than the standard height (5′ 6″) and chest-measurement. Sir Frank Souter also remarked that only 110 officers and 297 men, out of the whole force, were able to read and write, that no provision for their education existed, and that even if it were provided, the men were so overworked that they would be unable to take advantage of it. He urged the Government to sanction an immediate increase of 200 men in the lower ranks and to abolish the lowest grade of constable on Rs. 10 per month, on the ground that this was not a living wage and compared unfavourably with the salaries obtainable in private employ. The Bombay Government, while admitting the force of the Commissioner's arguments, declared that financial stringency prevented their granting the whole increase required and therefore sanctioned the cost of an additional 101 men, thus merely bringing the force up to the number declared to be necessary twenty years before.

The total strength and cost of the force during the last four years of Sir Frank Souter's *régime* were as follows:—

Year.	Number of all grades	Annual Cost
1885	1521	Rs. 475,297
1886	1580	„ 493,116
1887	1612	„ 510,690
1888	1621	„ 505,135

The small increase of 100 men between 1885 and 1888 was absurdly disproportionate to the extra burden of work entailed by the growth of the mill-industry, by the growing demands of the public, and by the activity of the legislature. Among the additional duties devolving on the Bombay police, which came prominently to notice after 1865, were the supervision of the weights and measures used by retail merchants and the prosecution of those whose weights did not conform to the official standard. In 1873, 112 shop-keepers were prosecuted for this offence and all except six were convicted. A year later Government commented unfavourably on the small number of prosecutions under the Arms Act and instructed the Commissioner to exercise a much stricter supervision over the importation and unlicensed sale of arms and ammunition. The Contagious Diseases Act, which no longer exists, was also the source of much extra work and fruitless trouble. In 1884 the Commissioner reported that there were 1435 women on the register, and ten years later 1500. "I regret to say" he wrote in the course of a report submitted in the former year, "that in the existing state of the law the efforts of the Police to control contagious diseases are almost futile. Hundreds of women, who are well known to be carrying on prostitution in the most open manner, cannot be registered because Magistrates require evidence which it is next to impossible to obtain." He added that the working of the Act involved a great deal of unnecessary expense, that the police were unable to discharge their duties satisfactorily, and that unless the hands of both the magistrates and the police were strengthened, it would be wiser to abolish the Act altogether. This view eventually found favour and, combined with strong pressure from other quarters, led to the abolition of the Act in July, 1888. A special staff of two officers and ten constables were released from an unpleasant task and were absorbed into the regular police force.

In 1884 occurs the earliest reference by the Commissioner to a matter which was destined to give him and his successors much additional work, namely the Haj or annual Muhammadan pilgrimage to Mecca. The number of pilgrims passing through Bombay had reached nearly 8,000, and had necessitated the appointment in 1882 of a Protector of Pilgrims and a regular system of passports. A Pilgrims Brokers' Act was also under consideration by the Indian legislature. Three years later, 1887, the task of issuing passports for Jeddah and selling steamer-tickets was entrusted to Messrs. Thomas Cook and Sons; but the success of this arrangement was discounted by the ignorance and helplessness of the pilgrims themselves, who failed to make full use of the facilities offered by the firm. The number of pilgrims passing annually through Bombay was far less than during the early years of the twentieth century: but their presence was nevertheless responsible for the building of one *musafirkhana* in Pakmodia street in 1871 and of another in Frere road in 1884. The growth of the Haj traffic before the outbreak of the Great War in 1914 added immensely to the volume of work annually devolving upon the Police Commissioner, and acquired additional importance from the political significance given to it by Indian Moslem agitators.

From time to time public interest was aroused during these years by sensational crimes. The earliest occurred in 1866, when four Europeans (3 Italians and an Austrian) murdered four Marwadis as they lay asleep in a house in Khoja Street. The motive of the crime was robbery; and the culprits were fortunately caught by the Deputy Commissioner, Mr. Edginton, and some European and Indian police, who pursued them from the scene of the crime. At the end of 1872 the Senior Magistrate of Police received information that a Parsi solicitor of the High Court and a Hindu accomplice had instigated a Fakir named Khaki Sha to kill one Nicholas de Ga and his wife by secret means for a reward of Rs. 5000. Similar information was also conveyed to Khan Bahadur Mir Akbar Ali, head of the detective police. Mr. R. H. Vincent, who was then acting Deputy Commissioner, Mir Akbar Ali, Mir Abdul Ali, Superintendent Mills and an European inspector concealed themselves behind a bamboo partition-wall in the Fakir's house in Kamathipura and thus overheard details of the plot against the de Gas. It transpired that Mrs. de Ga was entitled to certain property, of which the Parsi solicitor and a Mrs. Pennell were executors; and having mismanaged the property, the latter were anxious to obviate all chance of inquiry by the interested parties into their misconduct. The solicitor and his Hindu accomplice were both convicted. A curious case occurred in 1874, when Mr. James Hall of the Survey Department was accused of causing the death in Balasinor of three Indian troopers, attached to that department, and was adjudged at his trial to be of unsound mind. The murder of a European broker named Roonan by a European Portuguese, de Britto, in 1877 caused some temporary excitement, as also did a murder in the compound of H. H. the Aga Khan's house in Mazagon, perpetrated at a moment when most of the Khoja residents had gone to Byculla railway station to receive the corpse of the late Aga Ali Shah.

The last, and in some ways most interesting, case happened in November, 1888, when a Pathan strangled his wife, with the help of a friend, in a room in Pakmodia street. The two men placed the corpse of the woman in a box, tied up in sacking, and took it with a mattress on a cart to the neighbourhood of the Elphinstone Road railway station. There they left the box and mattress in charge of a cooly, telling him to watch them until they came back. They then walked into the city, where they sold the woman's jewellery and purchased tickets for Jeddah out of the proceeds. A day or two later they sailed together for the Hedjaz. The cooly, after waiting some time, took the box and mattress to his house, where they lay until November 23rd, three weeks after the murder. By that date the stench from the box was so overpowering that the cooly in alarm removed them to a dry ditch in the vicinity, where they were discovered by the police on November 24th. The woman's body was naturally so decomposed that identification was impossible. But by means of the box and the clothes of the deceased, Mir Abdul Ali and his men managed to trace the offenders, who were eventually arrested at Aden and brought back on December 10th to stand their trial.

Among other *causes célèbres* was the destruction of the *Aurora* in 1870, the morning after she had left Bombay, in pursuance of a conspiracy on the part of the master of the vessel and three other Europeans to defraud the underwriters by means of false bills-of-lading. The vessel was supposed to be laden with a heavy cargo of cotton which actually was never shipped. All the culprits, of whom two were ship and freight brokers in Bombay, were sentenced to long terms of penal servitude. Two interesting examples of the manufacture of false evidence occurred in 1872. In one case seven persons were charged with causing one Kuvarji Jetha to be stabbed by two men at Ahmedabad, in order that the fact of the stabbing might be adduced in evidence against a third party, against whom they bore a grudge; while in the second case three persons were convicted of robbery at Surat on evidence which the Bombay Police proved conclusively to have been manufactured by seven conspirators in Bombay. Two remarkable cases of cheque-forgeries by Parsis on the National and the Hong-Kong and Shanghai banks were committed to the Sessions in 1875.

The growth of intemperance was a noticeable feature of the period. In 1866-67, the Senior Magistrate, Mr. Barton, advocated more drastic restrictions on the sale of liquor, and in 1871 the Bombay Government commented upon the excessive prevalence of drinking, which was the immediate cause of twenty-one deaths in that year. In 1876 drunkenness was reported to have increased greatly among Indian women of the lower classes;[1] a further increase was reported in 1884, when 4,800 persons, including 224 Europeans, were charged with this offence; and in 1886 the total number of cases had risen to nearly 7,000. While the growth of a floating European population, connected with the harbour and shipping, certainly contributed to swell the returns of intemperance, the main causes underlying the increase were the rapid expansion of the textile industry and the growth of the industrial population, which, in the absence of facilities for decent recreation and in consequence of scandalous housing-conditions, was prone to drown its discomforts by resort to the nearest liquor-shop. Not a few of the problems, which still confront the Bombay executive authorities, can be traced back to this period when a large and important industry was suddenly developed by the genius and capacity of a number of Indian merchants, and a huge lower-class population, almost wholly illiterate and lacking moral and physical stamina, was introduced into the restricted area of the Island at a rate which defied all efforts to provide for its proper accommodation.

The growth of routine police-work during these years is apparent from the number of persons placed before the magisterial bench. Between 1874 and 1880 it increased from 21,500 to nearly 28,000, the exceptional number of 33,000, recorded in 1879, being due to the presence of a large body of immigrants, who had fled from the famine of the previous year in the Deccan and remained in Bombay in the hope of improving their condition by stealing. The volume of offences against property likewise expanded and would probably have been greater, but for the chances of steady employment afforded by the opening of new mills and the construction of dock works. Among the most unsatisfactory features of crime recorded during these years were the steady increase in the number of juvenile offenders and the comparatively large number of cases in which children

1. G. R. J. D. 2633 of April 21st, 1877.

were murdered for the sake of the gold and silver ornaments they were wearing. As Sir Frank Souter remarked, it is practically impossible for the State to provide an effective remedy for this evil, so long as Indian parents persist in a practice which offers overwhelming temptation to the criminal classes. The prosecution of persons for adultery, which is an offence under the Indian Penal Code, was another noteworthy feature of the crime records of the 'seventies. In 1872 nineteen, and in 1873 twenty-three offenders were prosecuted by the police for this offence, and all of them were acquitted. The extreme difficulty in a country like India of proving a criminal charge of this character led doubtless to the abandoment of such prosecutions in all but the rarest cases. A remarkable case of criminal breach of trust, in which no less than 51 separate charges were brought against a Parsi woman, who was convicted on three counts, and a clever theft of silver bars and coin from the Mint by some sepoys of the 10th Regiment N. I., owed their discovery to the detective abilities of the police.

The criminality of Europeans was due to specific causes connected with the growth of the port. As early as 1867 the prevalence of low freights and the difficulty of obtaining employment afloat or ashore led to much distress and crime among European seamen, and the Police were forced to undertake the task of finding work for some of this floating population and of shipping others to Europe. On the opening of the Suez Canal at the end of 1869, the old sailing vessels, in which the trade of the port had up to that date been carried on, yielded place to steamers, which remained only a short time in harbour and discharged and took in cargoes by steam-power. To this change in the shipping-arrangements was ascribed the prosecution in 1871 in the magisterial courts of 812 refractory sailors. A gradual improvement, however, took place in consequence of "the facilities of communication afforded

·by the telegraph", whereby "the amount of tonnage required for merchandize to be exported from Bombay to Europe can be regulated to a nicety. There are far fewer ships in the harbour seeking freight, while the crews of the Canal steamers being engaged for short periods and subject to only a brief detention in the port, the causes which produced discontent are not so prevalent as formerly."[1] Most of the European offenders, as is still the case, belonged to the sea-faring or military classes or to the fluctuating population of vagrants, and it was their conduct, not that of the regular European residents, which caused the proportion of offenders to the whole European population to compare very unfavourably with the proportion in other sects or communities. Much improvement of a permanent character resulted from the opening of the Sailors' Home by the Duke of Edinburgh in 1876, while from 1888 the police were relieved of the duty of prosecution in many cases by a decision of the magistracy that under the Mercantile Marine Act the police should no longer arrest European seamen summarily, but should leave the commanders of vessels to obtain process from the courts against defaulting members of their crews.

Only on three occasions was the public peace seriously broken during Sir Frank Souter's tenure of office. The first disturbance occurred in 1872 during the Muharram festival—the annual Muhammadan celebration of the deaths of Hasan and Husein, which up to the year 1912 offered an annual menace to law and order. Writing of this festival in 1885, Sir Frank Souter stated that it was always "a laborious and anxious time for the police, as until recent years it was almost certain to be ushered in by serious disturbances and often bloodshed, arising from the longstanding and at one time bitter feud existing between the Sunni and Shia sects. For many years it was found necessary to place a strong detachment of troops in the City, where they remained during the

1. G. R. J. D. 2427 of April 29th. 1873.

last two or three days of the Muharram, and it is only within the last few years that the usual requisition at the commencement of the Muharram to hold a party of military in readiness has been discontinued." By the middle of the 'eighties a better feeling existed between the two sects; but the excitement during the festival was still intense and the congregation in Bombay of Moslems from all parts of Asia rendered the work of the police extremely arduous. Apparently in 1872 the sectarian antagonism developed into open rioting, resulting in serious injury to about sixty people, before Sir Frank Souter gained control of the situation.[1] This outbreak was followed about a month later by a serious affray between two factions of the Parsi community outside the entrance to the Towers of Silence on Gibbs road. The police speedily put an end to the disturbance and arrested fifty persons for rioting, all of whom were subsequently acquitted by the High Court.[2]

These disturbances were trivial by comparison with the Parsi-Muhammadan riots of February, 1874, which ensued upon an ill-timed and improper attack upon the Prophet Muhammad, written and published by a Parsi in a daily newspaper. Shortly after 10 a. m. on the morning of February 13th, a mob of rough Muhammadans gathered outside the Jama Masjid, and after an exhortation by the Mulla began attacking the houses of Parsi residents. Two *agiaris* (fire-temples) were broken open and desecrated by a band of Sidis, Arabs and Pathans, who then commenced looting Parsi residences and attacking any Parsi whom they met on the road. One of the worst affrays occurred in Dhobi Talao. The Musalman burial-ground lies between the Queen's road and the Parsi quarter of that section, and an important Parsi fire-temple stands on the Girgaum road, which cuts the section from south to north. Alarmed at the approach of a large Muhammadan funeral

1. *Times of India*, 1872; Gazetteer of Bombay City and Island, II, 179.
2. Senior Magistrate's Report of Crime, 1873.

procession from the eastern side of the city, the Parsis threw stones at the Muhammadans, who retaliated, and a free fight with bludgeons and staves, in which many persons were injured, was carried on until the police arrived in force. Much damage to person and property was also done in Bhendy Bazar and the Khetwadi section.[1] On the following day the attitude of the Muhammadans was so threatening that the leading Parsis waited in a deputation on the Governor, Sir Philip Wodehouse, and begged him to send military aid to the Police, who appeared unable to cope with the situation. Sir Philip Wodehouse refused the request ; and when, in revenge for their losses some Parsis attacked a gang of Afghans near the Dadysett Agiari in Hornby road, the Governor summoned the leading Parsis and urged them to keep their co-religionists under better control. The hostility of the two communities, however, defied all efforts at conciliation, and in the end the troops of the garrison had to be called in to assist in the restoration of order.[2] The police eventually charged 106 persons with rioting, of whom 74 were convicted and sentenced to varying periods of imprisonment. During the progress of the riot, while the police were fully occupied in trying to restore order, the criminal classes took advantage of the situation and disposed of a large quantity of stolen property, which was never recovered.[3]

The Parsis were greatly dissatisfied with the attitude of the authorities and subsequently submitted a memorial to the Secretary of State, begging that an enquiry might be held into the rioting and blaming the police for apathy and the Government for not at once sending military assistance. The Governor's refusal to call out the troops, until the police were on the point of breaking down, was apparently due to his belief that his powers

1. *Times of India*, February 14th, 1874; the Annual Register, 1874; J. M. Maclean, *Guide to Bombay* (1902) p. 285 ; Gazetteer Bombay City II, 180.
2. Memoir of Sir Dinshaw Petit, Bart. by S. M. Edwardes, 1923.
3. Annual Report of Senior Magistrate, 1874.

in this direction were restricted. He was subsequently informed by Lord Salisbury that extreme constitutional theories could not safely be imported into India, and that therefore troops might legitimately be used to render a riot impossible.[1] The Secretary of State to this extent endorsed the views of the Parsi community, which felt that it had not been adequately protected.

Both before and after the passing of the Presidency Magistrates Act IV of 1877 the relations between the magistracy and the police were usually harmonious, and the court-work of the latter was much facilitated by the publication in February, 1881, of rules under that Act, designed to secure uniformity of practice in the four magistrates' courts and the better distribution and conduct of business. The question of delay caused by frequent adjournments to suit the convenience of barristers and pleaders, was also under consideration: and although no rules, however carefully framed, would suffice to prevent entirely the evil of procrastination, some amelioration was effected under the instructions and at the instance of the Bombay Government. The matter acquired added importance from the application to the Bombay courts on January 1st, 1883, of the provisions of the Criminal Procedure Code (Act X of 1882), which increased considerably the work of the Presidency Magistrates.

In 1887, the year preceding Sir Frank Souter's retirement and death, the Acting Chief Presidency Magistrate, Mr. Crawley Boevey, displayed a rather more critical attitude than had previously been customary towards the work of the police. He commented unfavourably upon the number of minor offences dealt with under the Police Act, and suggested that the Police sought to raise their percentages by charging large numbers of persons, some of whom were respectable residents, with trivial misdemeanours under local Acts, and that they

1. Letter from Lord Salisbury to the Governor-General in Council, July 9th, 1874.

Police Constable
Bombay City

might devote greater attention to the more serious forms of crime. At the same time Mr. Crawley Boevey evinced the strongest objection to the practice, hitherto followed as a precautionary measure by the constabulary, of searching suspicious characters at night; and he actually convicted and sentenced to a term of imprisonment an Indian constable who had arrested and searched a townsman in this way, under the authority given by section 35 of the old Police Act XIII of 1856. His decision was reversed on appeal by the High Court : but the practice, which had on several occasions led to the discovery of thefts and furnished clues to current investigations, was nevertheless temporarily abandoned, until Mr. Crawley Boevey had left the magisterial bench. It was resumed under Sir F. Souter's successor with the full concurrence of the Bombay Government, who recognized that the searching between midnight and 4-30 a. m. of wanderers who were unable to give a good account of themselves, was a valuable measure of precaution in both the prevention and detection of crime.

The Commissioner of Police remained responsible for the working of the Fire-Brigade practically up to the date of Sir Frank Souter's retirement. By 1887, however, the marked expansion of the city and the increase of police-work proper obliged Government to relieve the European police of all fire-brigade duty. The engineers of the Brigade were transferred in that year to the Municipality, and in the following year the whole organization, composed of engineers, firemen, tindals, lascars, coachmen and grooms, became an integral part of the municipal staff under the provisions of the new Municipal Act III of 1888. One of the largest fires dealt with by the Police, prior to the transfer, occurred in 1882, when the Oriental Spinning and Weaving Company's mill at Colaba, which dated from 1858, was completely destroyed.

The detective branch of the police-force, which was the nucleus of the modern C. I. D., was a creation of this period. Forjett, as has already been mentioned in connection with the events of 1857, had founded this department ; but his own powers and activities as a detective resulted in little attention being paid to the plain-clothes men who served under his immediate orders. When Sir Frank Souter succeeded him, the progress of the city in every direction demanded administrative capacity rather than detective ability in the Commissioner; and apart from the fact that no Englishman at the head of the force could hope to emulate Forjett's personal success as a detective, the increasing volume of routine work would in any case have obliged the holder of the office to delegate the special detection of crime to a picked body of his subordinates. The detective branch first came prominently to notice in 1872, in connexion with the de Ga and False Evidence cases mentioned in an earlier paragraph. At that date the head of the branch was Khan Bahadur Mir Akbar Ali. He was assisted by a more remarkable man, Khan Bahadur Mir Abdul Ali, who eventually succeeded him. Under their auspices the branch attained remarkable efficiency and was instrumental in unravelling many complicated cases of serious crime, such as the murder of the Pathan woman in 1887, and in breaking-up many gangs of thieves and house-breakers. Not the least important of their duties was the constant supply of information to the Commissioner of the state of public feeling in the City, and the exercise of a vigilant and tactful control over the inflammable elements among the masses at such seasons of excitement as the Muharram.

If it is true that a really successful detective is born and not made, Sir Frank Souter must be accounted fortunate in securing the services of two such men as Mir Akbar Ali and Mir Abdul Ali, of whom the latter wielded a degree of control over the *badmashes* of the City wholly disproportionate to his position as the superintendent of the *safed kapadawale* or plain-clothes police. Among his ablest assistants at the date of Sir Frank

Souter's retirement were Superintendent Harry Brewin, who was likewise destined to leave his mark upon the criminal administration, Inspector Framji Bhikaji, and Inspector Khan Saheb Roshan Ali Asad Ali. None of these men could be described as highly educated, and the majority of the native officers and constables under their orders were wholly illiterate: but they possessed great natural intelligence and acumen, an extraordinary *flair* for clues, and indefatigable energy. These qualities enabled them to solve problems, to which at first there seemed to be no clue whatever, and to keep closely in touch by methods of their own with the more disreputable and dangerous section of the urban population. It was for his services as Superintendent of the Detective Branch that Khan Bahadur Mir Abdul Ali was rewarded by Government in 1891 with the title of Sirdar.

From time to time the arrival of distinguished visitors threw an additional strain upon the police; and much of the success of the arrangements on these occasions must be attributed to the energy of the Deputy Commissioners of Police and the European Superintendents of the force. At the commencement of this period the Deputy Commissioner was Mr. Edginton, who had served under Mr. Forjett and shared with him the burdens of 1857. In 1865 he was deputed to England to qualify himself for the office of chief of a steam fire-brigade, then about to be introduced into Bombay, and he is mentioned as acting Commissioner of Police in 1874. During a further period of furlough in 1872, his place was taken by Mr. R. H. Vincent, and in 1884 permanently by Mr. Gell, both of whom were destined subsequently to succeed to the command of the force. Among the occasions demanding special police arrangements were the visit of the Viceroy, Lord Northbrook, in 1872, of the Duke of Edinburgh in 1870, of the Prince of Wales in 1875, of the Duke and Duchess of Connaught in 1883, the departure of Lord Ripon in 1884 and the Jubilee celebrations of 1887. The general character of the police administration is well illustrated by the statement of Sir Richard Temple (Governor of Bombay, 1877-80) that "the police, under the able management of Sir Frank Souter, was a really efficient body and popular withal,"[1] and by the words of Mr. C. P. Cooper, Senior Magistrate of Police, in 1875 that "during the time H. R. H. the Prince of Wales was in Bombay (November, 1875), when the City was much crowded with Native Chiefs and their followers, and by people from many parts of India, and when all the officers of the Department were on duty nearly the whole of the day and night, the Magistrates had, if any thing, less work than on ordinary occasions. This result was due to excellent police arrangements."[2] These eulogies were rendered possible by the hard work of successive Deputy Commissioners and of the non-gazetted officers of the police force.

Apart from the numerical inadequacy of the force, to which reference has already been made, the most vital needs during the later years of Sir Frank Souter's administration were the provision of police-buildings and the proper housing of the rank and file. In his reports for 1885 and 1886 the Commissioner explained that all except a fractional proportion of the constabulary were living in crowded and insanitary *chals*, the rent of the rooms which they occupied being much in excess of the monthly house allowance of one rupee, granted at that date to the lower ranks. The absence of sanitary barracks or lines was one of the chief reasons for the high percentage of men in hospital, and, coupled with the arduous duty demanded of a greatly undermanned force, had led directly to a decline in recruitment. The European police were in no better plight. In default of suitable official quarters they were forced to reside in cramped and inconvenient rooms, the owners of which were constantly raising the rents to a figure

1. Sir R. Temple, *Men & Events of My Time in India.*
2. Annual Report of Senior Magistrate of Police for 1875.

much higher than the monthly house allowance which the officers drew from the Government treasury. In some cases it was quite impossible for an officer to find accommodation in the area or section to which he was posted, and the discomfort was aggravated by his being obliged, in the absence of a proper police-station, to register complaints and interview parties in a portion of the verandah of his hired quarters. Some relief was afforded by the construction between 1871 and 1881 of the police-stations at Bazar Gate, facing the Victoria Terminus, and at Paidhoni, which commands the entrance to Parel road (Bhendy Bazar) : while from 1868 the police were allowed the partial use of the old Maharbaudi building in Girgaum, which served for twenty-five years as the Court of the Second Magistrate.

In 1885 the Bombay Government sanctioned the building of a new Head Police Office opposite the Arthur Crawford market. This work, however, was not commenced till the end of 1894, and the building was not occupied till 1899; and meantime the Commissioner annually urged upon Government the need of adding barracks for the constabulary to the proposed head-quarters, on the grounds that the chosen site was far more convenient than that of the old police office (built in 1882) and lines at Byculla, both for keeping in touch with the pulse of the City and for concentrating reinforcements during seasons of popular excitement and disturbance. Further relief for the European police was also secured in 1888 by the completion of the Esplanade Police Court, which superseded an old and unsuitable building in Hornby road, occupied for many years by the courts of the Senior and Third Magistrates. Quarters for a limited number of European police officers were provided on the third floor of the new building, which was opened in May, 1889.

Thus, apart from the task of perfecting arrangements for the prevention and detection of crime on the foundations laid by Sir Frank Souter, the chief problem which his successors inherited was the proper housing of the police force, in a city where overcrowding and insanitation had become a public scandal. The inconvenient and unpleasant conditions in which the police were obliged to perform their daily duties resulted directly from the phenomenal growth of Bombay since the year 1860, and from the inability of the Government to allot sufficient funds for keeping the police administration abreast of the social and commercial development of the city. During his long *régime* of twenty-four years Sir Frank Souter saw the extension of the B. B. and C. I. Railway to Bombay, the opening of regular communication by rail with the Deccan and Southern Maratha Country, the construction of the Suez Canal and the appearance in Bombay of six or seven European steamship-companies, the feverish prosecution of reclamation of land from the sea, which increased the area of the Island from 18 to 22 square miles, the construction of many new roads and overbridges, the building of great water-works, the projection of drainage schemes, and the lighting of the streets with gas. He witnessed the old divisions of the Island develop into municipal wards and sections; saw the opening of the Prince's, Victoria and Merewether docks; saw the first tramway lines laid in 1872, and watched the once rural area to the north of the Old Town develop into the busy industrial sections of Tardeo, Nagpada, Byculla, Chinchpugli and Parel. The number of cotton-spinning and weaving mills increased from 10 in 1870 to 70 at the date of his retirement, and the urban population increased *pari passu* with this expansion of trade and industrial enterprise. Between 1872 and 1881 the population increased from 644,405 to 773,196, and by 1888 it cannot have been much less than 800,000.

Sir Frank Souter relinquished his office on April 30th, 1888, and retired to the Nilgiris in the Madras Presidency, where he died in the following July. Thus ended a remarkable epoch in the annals of the Bombay

Police. It says much for the administrative capacity of the Commissioner that, in spite of an inadequate police-force and the difficulties alluded to in a previous paragraph, he was able to cope successfully with crime and maintain the peace of the City unbroken for fourteen years. Frequent references in their reviews of his annual reports show that the Bombay Government fully realized the valuable character of his services, while the confidence which he inspired in the public is proved by the testimony of trained observers like Sir Richard Temple, by the great memorial meeting held in Bombay after his death, at which Sir Dinshaw Petit moved a resolution of condolence with his family, and by the erection of the marble bust which still adorns the council-hall of the Municipal Corporation. His own subordinates, both European and Indian, regretted his departure perhaps more keenly than others, for he occupied towards them an almost patriarchal position. All ranks had learnt by long experience to appreciate his vigour and determination and his even-handed justice, which, while based upon a high standard of efficiency and integrity, was not blind to the many temptations, difficulties and discouragements that beset the daily life of an Indian constable. Realizing how much he had done to advance their interests and secure their welfare during nearly a quarter of a century, the Police Force paid its last tribute of respect to the Commissioner by subscribing the cost of the marble bust by Roscoe Mullins, which stands in front of the main entrance of the present Head Police Office.

The memory of Sir Frank Souter is likely to endure long after the last of the men who served under him has earned his final discharge, for he was gifted with a personality which impressed itself upon the imagination of all those who came in contact with him. More than twenty years after his death, the writer of this book watched an old and grizzled Jemadar turn aside as he left the entrance of the Head Police Office and halt in front of the bust. There he drew himself smartly to attention and gravely saluted the marble simulacrum of the dead Commissioner—an act of respect which illustrated more vividly than any written record the personal qualities which distinguished Sir Frank Souter during his long and successful career in India.

LIEUT.-COLONEL W. H. WILSON

CHAPTER V

LIEUT.-COLONEL W. H. WILSON
1888—1893

Lieut-Colonel W. H. Wilson, who belonged to the Bombay District Police, succeeded Sir Frank Souter on July 4th, 1888. He had already acted once as Commissioner from October 1885 to May 1886, during his predecessor's absence on furlough. During the period which intervened between Sir F. Souter's departure on April 30th and Colonel Wilson's appointment in July, the duties of the Commissioner devolved upon Mr. H. G. Gell, the Deputy Commissioner. Colonel Wilson held the appointment for five years, during which he was twice absent on leave, once from May to December, 1889, when Colonel Wise was appointed *locum tenens*, and again for three months in 1890, when his place was filled by Major Humfrey.

Throughout his term of office Colonel Wilson, like his predecessor, was hampered by lack of men. The force at the date of his assumption of control numbered 1621 and cost annually Rs. 505,135. By 1892 there had been a trivial increase to 1634, while the annual cost had risen to Rs. 513,896. This lack of men was undoubtedly responsible for a decline in the prevention and detection of crime, as for example in 1888, when many cases of house-breaking were undetected, and in 1891, when a serious increase of crime against property was recorded in Mahim and other outlying areas. It also resulted in the force being so seriously overworked that the percentage of men admitted to hospital showed a constant tendency to increase. In his report of 1892 Colonel Wilson informed Government that the burden of duty sustained by the rank and file had become almost intolerable, that the men frequently became prematurely aged from overwork, and that many of the superior officers were ill from exposure and lack of rest. The Bombay Government endorsed the Commissioner's complaints and admitted the urgent need of increasing the Force.[1] A reorganization of the Force, involving a considerable addition to its numbers, had in fact been under consideration for several years; but owing partly to financial stringency and partly to the delay inseparable from all official transactions, the much-needed relief was not granted until August, 1893,[2] by which date Colonel Wilson had left India and Mr. Vincent had taken his place. The former thus had little or no chance of securing any improvement in the criminal work of the divisional police, and on more than one occasion he found his force singularly inadequate to cope with special and emergent duties.

Like Sir Frank Souter, he also found the lack of police-stations and buildings a serious obstacle to efficient administration. Within a few months of assuming office he reported that the building at Byculla, in which he worked, was very inconvenient and too far distant from the business quarters of the City, and he urged the early construction of the proposed Head Police Office on Hornby road. He reiterated his demands in 1890, 1891, and 1892, stating that no real improvement could be effected until that office and additional quarters for the men were constructed. As mentioned in the preceding chapter, accommodation was provided for two European police officers in the Esplanade Police Court, which was occupied for the first time in 1889; while in the last year of his tenure of office, the divisional police secured some extra accommodation by the full use of the old Maharbaudi building, which had proved inconvenient to the public and was therefore vacated in 1893 by the Second Presidency Magistrate in favour of a Government building in Nesbit Lane, Mazagon.[3]

1. G. R. J. D., June 24th. 1892.
2. G. R. J. D., 5389 of August 28th. 1893.
3. Gazetteer of Bombay City and Island, II, 237. A Fourth Presidency Magistrate was appointed in 1892 and was accommodated

In the latter building also accommodation was provided for two European police officers.

The capabilities of the detective police were tested by several serious crimes. The first, known as the Dadar Triple Murder, occurred in 1888 and aroused considerable public interest. Two Parsi women and a little boy, residing in Lady Jamshedji road, were brutally murdered by a Hindu servant, who was in due course traced, tried and executed. In 1890 the murder of a Hindu youth at Clerk Road was successfully detected, and this was followed in 1891 by the Khambekar Street poisoning case, in which a respectable and wealthy family of Memons were killed by a dissolute son of the house. The police investigation, which ended in the trial and conviction of the murderer, was greatly obstructed by the collateral relatives of the family, who made every effort to render the enquiry abortive and were actively assisted by the whole Memon community.

These crimes, however, were cast into the shade by the famous Rajabai Tower case, which caused great public agitation. On April 25th, 1891, two Parsi girls, Pherozebai and Bacchubai, aged respectively 16 and 20 years, were found lying at the foot of the Rajabai Clock Tower, in circumstances and under conditions which indicated that they had been thrown from above. When discovered, one of the girls was dead, and the other so seriously injured that she expired within a few minutes. Suspicion fell upon a Parsi named Manekji and certain other persons: but the latter were released shortly after arrest, as there was no evidence that they were in any way concerned in the death of the two girls. The Coroner's jury, after nineteen sittings, gave a verdict that Bacchubai had thrown herself from the tower in consequence of an attempted outrage upon her by some person or persons unknown, and that Manekji was privy

in the Esplanade Police Court. After the occupation of the Nesbit Lane building by the Second Presidency Magistrate, the Court of the Fourth Magistrate was also located there.

to the attempted outrage; and further that Pherozebai had been thrown from the tower by Manekji, in order to prevent her giving information of the attempt to outrage herself and her friend. Manekji was tried by the High Court on a charge of murder and was acquitted. Various rumours were afloat as to the identity of the chief actors in the crime, among those suspected being a young Muhammadan belonging to a leading Bombay family. No further clue was ever obtained, and to this day the true facts are shrouded in mystery.

The police dealt successfully with an important case of forgery, in which counterfeit stamps of the value of one rupee were very cleverly forged by a man who had previously served in the Trigonometrical Survey Department of the Government of India and was afterwards proved to have belonged to a gang of expert forgers in Poona. The collapse of a newly-built house prompted Superintendent Brewin to make a lengthy and careful inquiry into all the details of construction, which ended successfully in the prosecution and punishment of the two jerry-builders who erected it. House-collapses are not unknown in Bombay, particularly during the monsoon, when the weight of the wet tiles causes the posts of wooden-frame dwellings to give way; but so far as is known, the case quoted is the only instance on record of a builder being prosecuted and punished under the criminal law for causing loss of life by careless or defective construction. The Sirdar Abdul Ali was equally successful in unravelling an important case of illicit traffic in arms and ammunition carried on by a gang of Pathans with certain transfrontier outlaws—a matter in which the Government of India at that date (1888) took considerable interest.

The offence of gambling in various forms occupied the attention of the police to a greater degree than before, and the prevalence of rain-gambling led to a test prosecution in the magisterial courts. This form of wagering used to take place during the monsoon at Paidhoni, where a house would be rented at a high price for the four months of the rains by a group of Indian capitalists. There were two forms of *Barsat ka satta* or rain-gambling, known familiarly as *Calcutta mori* and *Lakdi satta*. In the former case wagers were laid as to whether the rain would percolate in a fixed time through a specially prepared box filled with sand, the bankers settling the rates or odds by the appearance and direction of the clouds. In the latter case, winnings or losses depended on whether the rainfall during a fixed period of time was sufficient to fill the gutter of a roof and overflow. The gambling took place usually between 6 a.m. and 12 noon, and again between 6 p.m. and midnight, the rates varying according to the appearance of the sky and the time left before the period open for the booking of bets expired. The practice, which was very popular, was responsible for so much loss that in 1888 two of the principal promoters of rain-gambling were prosecuted by the order of Government. The Chief Presidency Magistrate, Mr. Cooper, who tried the case, decided that rain-gambling was not an offence under the Gambling Act, as then existing, and his decision was upheld on appeal by the High Court. Consequently Colonel Wilson applied for the necessary amendment of the Bombay Gambling Act, and this was in due course effected by the Legislature. Since that date rain-gambling has been unknown in Bombay.

In 1890 and 1891 the police made continual raids on gambling-houses, and in 1893 were obliged to adopt special measures against a form of bagatelle, known as *Eki beki*, which had a wide vogue in the City. The Public Prosecutor himself visited one of the more notorious resorts in order to acquaint himself thoroughly with the system, which in consequence of continuous action by the police was for the time being practically stamped out of existence. Bombay, however, has always been addicted to gambling, whether it be in the form of the well-known *teji-mundi* contracts, the *ank satta* or opium-gambling, or the ordinary gambling with dice and cards: and notwithstanding that the police at intervals pay special attention to the vice and secure some improvement, the evil reappears and rapidly increases, directly vigilance is relaxed. The promoters of gambling are adepts in the art of misleading the authorities: they rarely use the same room on two successive occasions; they have elaborated a vocabulary of warning-calls; and they employ spies and watchmen to keep them posted in all the movements of the police. Some of the latter have probably at times accepted hush-money and presents to turn a blind eye on the gamblers' movements: for otherwise it is difficult to understand why men, who are widely known to have been organizing gambling reunions for years, should have successfully evaded the law and in some cases have accumulated a considerable fortune in the process.

Two matters of a novel character engaged the attention of the divisional police during Colonel Wilson's *régime*. The first was a series of balloon ascents, which drew immense crowds of spectators. The earliest ascents were performed in the opening months of 1889 from the grounds of old Government House, Parel, by a Mr. Spencer, who successfully descended with a parachute. He was followed in 1891 by Mr. and Mrs. Van Tassell, who, except on one occasion when the lady's parachute did not open immediately, carried out their performances without a hitch. This form of public amusement, however, came to a sudden and unhappy conclusion on December 10th, 1891, when Lieutenant Mansfield, R. N., essayed an ascent. When he had reached a height of about 1000 feet, the balloon suddenly burst, and he fell headlong to earth and was killed in full view of a large crowd of spectators. Since that date and up to the outbreak of the War in 1914, the only aerial spectacle offered to the Bombay public was a much-advertised aeroplane flight from the Oval. This venture was a fiasco. The aeroplane would only rise a few feet from the ground, and at that elevation collided violently with the iron railing of the B. B. and C. I. railway and was wrecked.

The second event, which evoked much comment, was a strike by the *employés* of eleven cotton-spinning mills as a protest against a reduction in wages. So far as can be gathered from official records, this was the first strike of any magnitude that occurred in the industrial area, and seems to have been the earliest effort of the labour-population to test their powers of combination. The police had to be concentrated in the affected area, in order to guard mill-property and quell possible disorder: but the mill-workers at this date were quite unorganized and no disturbance occurred. The action of these mill-hands, however, carried the germ of the disorders which have since caused periodical damage to the industry and have interfered frequently with the normal duties of the police force.

It is convenient at this point to refer to the problem of European prostitution, which has repeatedly formed the subject of comment in more recent years. Before the opening of the Suez Canal in 1869, the foreign prostitute from eastern Europe was practically unknown in Bombay, and such immorality as existed was confined to women of Eurasian or Indian parentage. Once, however, the large European shipping-companies had established regular steamer-communication with India, and Port Said had become a port of call and an asylum for the riff-raff of Europe, the Jew procurer and "white-slave" trafficker gradually included India within the orbit of a trade, which was characterized by a fairly regular demand and by large and easily earned profits. The Foreigners Act III of 1864, under the provisions of which the Bombay Police arrange for the deportation of foreign pimps, as well as of prostitutes whose conduct demands their expulsion, was apparently not used frequently before the last decade of the nineteenth century, except against troublesome Pathans and Arabs, belonging respectively to the transfrontier region or to the territory of Indian Princes. But the immigration of foreign women must have begun tentatively during the *régime* of Sir Frank Souter and continued to expand under the auspices of the international procurer, until by the last years of the nineteenth century these unfortunates had secured a strong foothold in certain houses situated in Tardeo, Grant road and other streets of the Byculla ward.

The growth of the European population, resulting from the expansion of the trade of the port, and an increasing disinclination on the part of Government and society to countenance the old system of *liaisons* with Indian women, may have induced the authorities to regard the establishment of the European brothel and the presence of the European prostitute as deplorable but necessary evils. Provided that the women were kept under reasonable control and the police were sufficiently vigilant to ensure the non-occurrence of open scandals, no direct steps were taken to abolish a feature of urban life which struck occasional travellers and others as inexpressibly shocking. To the peripatetic procurer, who visited Bombay at frequent intervals in order to relieve the women of their savings and ascertain the demand for fresh arrivals, the Police showed no mercy; and the regular use which they made of the Foreigners Act towards the close of the last century indicates that by that date Bombay (like Calcutta and Madras) had become a regular halting-point in the procurer's disgraceful itinerary from Europe to the Far East.

It must be remembered that the number of European professional prostitutes in India has never been large, and the worst features of the traffic, as understood in Europe, are fortunately absent. That is to say, the women of this class who find their way to the brothels of the Grant Road neighbourhood and to the less secluded rooms in and around the notorious Cursetji

'Suklaji street, which used to be known on this account as *safed gali* or "white lane", are not decoyed thither by force or fraud. The women usually arrive unaccompanied and of their own choice, and they are well over the age of majority before they first set foot on the Bombay *bandar*. Their treatment in the brothel is not bad and they are not subjected to cruelty. The "mistress" of the brothel, who is herself a time-expired prostitute and has sometimes paid a heavy sum to her predecessor for the good-will of the house, feeds and houses the women in return for 50 per cent of their daily earnings; and as her own livelihood and capital are at stake, she is usually careful to see that nothing occurs to give the house a bad name among her clientèle or to warrant punitive action on the part of the police. The "mistress" acts in fact as a buffer between the women of her house and the male visitor, protecting the general interests and health of the former and safeguarding the latter from theft and robbery by the women, who are usually drawn from the lower strata of the population of eastern Europe and who would, in the absence of such control, be liable to thieve and quarrel, and would also commence visiting places of public resort, such as the race-course, restaurants etc., and walking the streets of the European quarter.

European women of this class are found only in the chief maritime cities of India—Calcutta, Bombay, Madras, Karachi and Rangoon, the only places in India which contain a considerable miscellaneous European population. Their total number is not large. Some of them doubtless were originally victims of the "white-slave" trafficker; but their first initiation to the life happened several years before they found their way to India, with funds advanced to them by the pimp or, as they style him in their jargon, "the fancy-man" who first led them astray. There have been instances in Bombay of these women contriving to accumulate sufficient savings in the course of ten or twelve years' continuous prostitution to enable them either to purchase the good-will of a recognized brothel or to return to their own country and settle down there in comparative respectability. One or two, with their savings behind them, have been able to find a husband who was prepared to turn a blind eye to their past. Thus has lower middle-class respectability been secured at the price of years of flaming immorality. But such cases are rare. These women as a class are wasteful and improvident, and are prone to spend all their earnings on their personal tastes and adornment. Most of them also, as remarked above, have become acquainted early in their career with a procurer, usually a Jew of low type, who swoops down at intervals from Europe upon the brothel in which they happen to be serving and there relieves them of such money as they may have saved after paying the recognized 50 per cent to the " mistress " of the house.

During Colonel Wilson's Commissionership little mention is made of action by the police against the foreign procurer. The latter was probably not so much in evidence as he was at a later date. The opening years of the twentieth century witnessed a change, however, in this respect, and a short time before the outbreak of the Great War, the Government of India made a special enquiry into the scope and character of European prostitution in India, in consequence of the submission to the Imperial Legislature of a private Bill designed to suppress the evil. The report on the subject submitted at that date (1913) by the Commissioner of Police, Bombay, was directly responsible for a decision to give the police wider powers of control over the casual visits of European procurers—a decision which was carried into effect after the close of the War by strengthening the provisions of the local Police Act and the Foreigners Act. In 1921 the Government of India was represented at an International Conference on the Traffic in Women and Children, held at Geneva under the auspices of the League of

Nations; and shortly afterwards India became a signatory of the International Convention of 1910, by which all the States concerned bind themselves to carry out certain measures designed to check and ultimately to abolish the traffic.

There is little else to chronicle concerning the work of the police under Colonel Wilson. The arrangements for the visits of the late Prince Albert Victor and the Cesarewitch in 1890 were carried through without a hitch, despite the acknowledged inadequacy of the force. The annual Moslem pilgrimage to Mecca brought to Bombay yearly about 8000 pilgrims, whose passports and steamer-tickets were supplied by Messrs. Thomas Cook and Sons, the general supervision of the pilgrims and their embarkation at the docks being performed by the Protector of Pilgrims and a small staff, in collaboration with the Port Health officer. The period was remarkable for the establishment of several temperance movements in various parts of the City, which were declared in 1891 to have imposed a check upon wholesale drunkenness. No diminution, however, of the volume of crime against property was recorded, despite the activities of the Detective Branch and the action taken by the divisional police against receivers of stolen property, of whom 80 were convicted in 1889 and 64 in the following year. The property annually recovered by the police in cases of theft and house-breaking amounted to about 50 per cent of the value stolen, the paucity of the constabulary being the chief reason for the non-detection of constant thefts and burglaries which occurred in Mahim and other outlying areas. Considering how greatly he was handicapped by lack of numbers, ill-health among the rank and file, and the absence of proper accommodation for both officers and men, Colonel Wilson's administration may be said to have been fairly successful. Fortunately he was spared the task of dealing with any serious outbreak of disorder, such as occurred during the early days of his successor's term of office.

CHAPTER VI

Mr. R. H. Vincent, C.I.E.

1893—1898

When Colonel Wilson left Bombay for England in April, 1893, his place was taken by Mr. R. H. Vincent, who had previously acted as Deputy Commissioner for a few months in 1872. A foreigner by birth, Mr. Vincent had served in his youth in the Foreign Legion of Garibaldi's army. He came subsequently to India and obtained an appointment in the Bombay District Police, in which his linguistic faculties and general capacity soon marked him out for promotion. He was appointed Acting Commissioner in April and was confirmed in the appointment shortly afterwards, when Colonel Wilson sent in his papers. His five years of office were remarkable for two grave outbreaks of disorder, one of them being the most serious riot that ever occurred in Bombay, for the outbreak of plague, which threw an enormous extra strain upon the police-force, and thirdly for the initiation by political agitators of the public Ganpati festivals, which supplied a direct incitement to sedition and disorder.

A reorganization of the police-force was finally sanctioned by Government in an order of August 28th, 1893, in consequence whereof the strength of the force at the close of that year was reported to be 1831, exclusive of 99 harbour police paid for by the Port Trustees. The extra number of men, coupled with revised rates of pay and allowances, brought the annual cost of the force to Rs. 518,078. A further addition to the force was sanctioned at the beginning of 1894, the net increase of men enlisted during that year being 287, of whom five were Europeans, fourteen were native officers, and fifty-three were mounted police.

Mr. R. H. VINCENT

The armed police were augmented by 66 men and the unarmed by 140, including 15 European and 11 Indian officers. The mounted police were placed under the command of an Inspector named Sheehy, specially recruited from a British cavalry regiment. In consequence of these additions, the Commissioner at the close of 1894 was in command of a total force (exclusive of the harbour police) of 2111, costing annually Rs. 710,528. The harbour police were also increased to 114 in 1895.

Excluding a small body of seven constables recruited in 1896 for special duty under the Glanders and Farcy Act, the sanctioned strength and cost of the force remained unaltered during the last three years of Mr. Vincent's term of office. The number, though more adequate than in Colonel Wilson's time, was yet barely sufficient to cope with all the duties imposed upon the force, while the advent of the plague and other events aggravated the strain. During the decade following upon Mr. Vincent's retirement appeals for more men were followed by spasmodic additions to the force until the publication in 1905 of the report of the Police Commission appointed by Lord Curzon. This resulted in a thorough scrutiny of the various police administrations and led in the case of Bombay to the preparation of a new and radical scheme of reform.

In the matter of crime, the period of Mr. Vincent's Commissionership was remarkable for several murders, fifteen of which occurred in the year 1893. One of the most sensational crimes was the "double murder" at Walkeshwar in April 1897, when a Bhattia merchant and his sister were killed in a house near the temple by a gang of six men, all of whom were traced and arrested by the police after a protracted and difficult investigation. Five of the culprits were eventually hanged. The police were also successful in 1893 in breaking up two gangs of *dhatura*-poisoners, who had robbed a large number of people. In 1895 Superintendent Brewin, with the help of the Sirdar Abdul Ali and his detectives, successfully unravelled a case of poisoning, perpetrated with the object of defrauding the Sun Life Assurance Company. A Goanese named Fonseca insured the life of a friend, Duarte, with the company and shortly afterwards administered to him a dose of arsenic, which he had obtained from a European employed in Stephens' stables, who used the poison for killing rats. Prior to insuring Duarte's life, Fonseca had him medically examined by two Indian Christian doctors of Portuguese descent, well-known in Bombay, who made a very perfunctory examination. Subsequently, when Fonseca asked them to certify the cause of Duarte's death, they acted even more negligently and gave a certificate of death from natural causes without any inquiry. Certain facts, however, aroused the suspicions of the manager of the Assurance Company; the police were called in; and in due course Fonseca was tried and convicted of murder.

The records of 1893 mention the arrest and conviction of a leading member of the famous *Sonari Toli* or Golden Gang of swindlers, which for some time made a lucrative livelihood by fleecing the more credulous section of the public. But in the case of ordinary theft and robbery the police were less successful in recovering stolen property than in previous years, the percentage of recovery for the five years ending in 1894 being only 48 and declining to 35 in 1898. Much of this crime was committed by professional bad characters and members of criminal tribes belonging to the Deccan and other parts of the Bombay Presidency. The prevalence of robbery and theft was viewed with such dissatisfaction by the Bombay Government that in 1894 they urged the Commissioner to make use of the provisions of chapter VIII of the Criminal Procedure Code, which had been applied with much success in up-country districts. Unfortunately the Bombay magistracy required as a rule far more direct evidence of bad livelihood than was procurable by the urban police, and any regular use of that chapter of the Code was therefore declared by the Commissioner to be impracticable.

The court-work of the police under the local Act was indirectly affected by the closing of the opium-dens of the City in 1893. This was one result of the appointment in that year of a Parliamentary Commission to inquire into the extent of opium consumption in India, its effects on the physique of the people, and the suggestion that the sale of the drug should be prohibited except for medicinal purposes. In consequence of the anti-opium agitation in England, the consumption of opium was from that date permitted only on a small scale in one or two "clubs" in the City, frequented by the lower classes. The opponents of the practice did not foresee that opium-smoking cannot be entirely abolished by laws and regulations, and that the stoppage of supplies of the drug merely results in the public seeking other more disastrous forms of self-indulgence. In Bombay the closing of the opium-shops led directly to a great increase of drunkenness,[1] and a few years later to the far more pernicious and degrading habit of cocaine-eating. The experience of most Bombay police-officers is that the smoking of opium does not *per se* incite men to commit crime, and when practised in moderation it does not prevent a man from performing his daily work. Cocaine on the other hand destroys its victims body and soul, and the confirmed cocaine-eater usually develops into a criminal, even if he was not one previously.

The practice of affixing bars to the ground-floor rooms in Duncan road, Falkland road and neighbouring lanes, occupied by the lowest class of Indian prostitutes, is usually supposed to have been introduced during the period of. Mr. Vincent's Commissionership. Strangers who visit Bombay, as well as respectable European and Indian residents,

1. Report of Comm. of Police for 1893.

are apt to be shocked by the sight of these Mhar, Dhed and other low-caste women sitting behind bars, like caged animals, in rooms opening directly on the street. It is not, however, generally known that the bars were put up, not for the purpose of what has been styled "exhibitionism", but in order to save the woman from being overwhelmed by a low-class male rabble, ready for violence on the smallest provocation. Before the women barred the front of their squalid rooms, there were constant scenes of disorder, resulting occasionally in injuries to the occupants; and it was on the advice of the police that about this date the women had the bars affixed, which oblige their low-class clientèle to form a queue outside and enable the women to admit one customer at a time. Considering that a prostitute of this class charges only 4 annas for her favours and lives in great squalor, it is not surprising that venereal disease is extremely common, and that the offering of four annas to Venus ends generally in a further expenditure of one or two rupees on quack remedies.

As regards regular police-work, Mr. Vincent made an attempt in 1894 to improve the regulation of traffic on public thoroughfares. This was necessitated by the steady increase of the number of public and private conveyances, the former having risen from 5392 in 1884 to 8301 in 1894, and the latter at the same dates from 2674 to 5416. On the other hand the width of the roads had, with here and there occasional setbacks, remained constant for twenty years, and the majority of the streets were totally inadequate for the increased volume of daily traffic. The Commissioner's efforts to control traffic more effectively did result in a decrease of street-accidents, but they failed at the same time to meet with "the approval of the entire native community". Therein lies one of the chief obstacles to efficient traffic-regulation in Bombay. The ordinary Indian constable, though more able and alert than he used to be, is still a poor performer as a regulator of traffic. He is not likely to improve, so long as Indians persist in using the roads in the manner of their forefathers in rural towns and villages, and so long as he is doubtful of the support of the magistracy in cases where he prosecutes foot-passengers and cab-drivers for neglect of his orders and of the rule of the road. Apart also from the possibility of the constable not being supported by the bench, as he usually is in England, the great delays which are liable to occur in the hearing of these trivial cases, through the procrastination of pleaders for the defence, act as a direct discouragement to prosecutions. A real and permanent improvement in traffic conditions cannot be secured, until the Indian public develops "a traffic conscience" and insists upon the relinquishment of ancient and haphazard methods of progression inherited from past centuries.

In the same year (1894) the Commissioner reported that, in accordance with the orders of Government, he had introduced the Bertillon system of anthropometry at the Head Police Office, but he expressed a doubt whether results commensurate with the cost of working would be obtained. The following year he stated definitely that the system was a failure, but was urged by Government to persevere with it. The system, nevertheless, was doomed, and in 1896 was superseded by the far more accurate and successful finger-print system which was introduced into India by Mr. (afterwards Sir Edward) Henry, the Inspector-General of Police in Bengal. Although the Bertillon system was not finally abolished till the end of 1899, Mr. Vincent was able to report in 1898 that a finger-print bureau had been established, that two police officers had been deputed to Poona to learn from Mr. Henry himself the details of the system of criminal identification, and that by the end of the year 300 finger-impressions had been recorded. This was the origin of the Bombay City

Finger-Print bureau, which by steadily augmenting its own record of criminals and by interchange of slips with the larger Presidency bureau at Poona, has compiled a very useful reference-work for investigating officers.

The rapid extension of the scope of police work and the need of dealing more quickly and effectively with various classes of offences had for some time impressed upon the local authorities the need for a new police law. The old Act XLVIII of 1860, under which the police worked in the days of Mr. Forjett, had been followed by three successive Town Police Acts, Nos. I of 1872, II of 1879 and IV of 1882. But the provisions of these Acts needed amendment and consolidation to meet the altered conditions of later years; and the Commissioner was justified in saying, as he did in 1898, that the police were "working at a disadvantage and were hampered in many ways" by the want of a comprehensive and intelligible City Police Act, which would enable them to deal effectively with the investigation of crime and the arrest and detention of offenders and with the special offences peculiar to a large city. He expressed a hope that the new City Police Bill, which had been under the consideration of Government for several years, would be enacted without further delay. Four years were still to elapse before this hope was fulfilled by the passing of Bombay Act IV of 1902. In the meanwhile the police, as well as the magistrates,[1] had to perform their respective duties as best they could under the old law. Such success as the police achieved in dealing with crime and other evils was due largely to the energy and experience of the older Divisional Superintendents, such as Messrs. Crummy,[2] Ingram, Grennan, McDermott, Sweeney, Nolan and Brewin, of the Sirdar Mir Abdul Ali, and of tried Indian inspectors like Rao Saheb Tatya

1. Mr. Cooper, the Chief Presidency Magistrate, retired in 1893 and was succeeded by Mr. J. Sanders-Slater.

2 Mr. Crummy acted more than once as Deputy Commissioner of Police.

KHAN BAHADUR SHEIKH IBRAHIM SHEIKH IMAM

Joined the Force, 1864—Retired, 1911

Lakshman, Khan Saheb Roshan Ali and Khan Saheb (afterwards Khan Bahadur) Sheikh Ibrahim Sheikh Imam.

Mr. Vincent's term of office was marked by the first outbreak of plague in the later months of 1896. When the disease first assumed epidemic form, there was a wild panic among all classes, and people fled in crowds from the city, leaving their homes unoccupied and unprotected. This led for the time being to a large increase of offences against property, committed by professional bad characters who took immediate advantage of the general exodus. The decrease of police cases in 1897 was due solely to the fact that the constant demands upon the force for duties connected with plague-inspection and segregation etc., left them no leisure to deal with the criminal classes, who throughout the early days of the epidemic indulged in an orgy of theft and house-breaking. It was estimated in February, 1897, that 400,000 inhabitants had fled from the city, most of whom left their houses entirely unprotected. The Bombay Government was faced with "a difficult and delicate problem—the extent to which it was possible in view of Indian prejudices and convictions to put into force the scientific counsels of perfection pressed upon them by their medical advisers. The doctors drew up plans for house-to-house visitation, disinfection, isolation hospitals, segregation-camps, and inoculation, all of which were intensely distasteful to the Indian population with their caste regulations and their jealousy of any infringement of privacy in their home life."[1]

The police were constantly requisitioned to assist in one way or another the official attempts to stamp out the epidemic, and considering the extra strain thrown upon them by the various plague-preventive measures, it is surprising that they managed to cope as effectively as they did with their regular duties. In 1897 Mr. Rand of the Indian Civil Service and Lieutenant Ayerst, who had

1. P. E. Roberts, *Hist. Geography of British Dependencies*, Vol. VII, p. 508.

been engaged on plague-work, were assassinated at Poona. In connexion with the inquiry which followed Superintendent Brewin was summoned from Bombay and placed on special duty in Poona. In the following year occurred the plague-riots, to which reference will be made in a later paragraph. The difficulties which confronted the police during the first two or three years of the plague epidemic were aggravated by the unscrupulous campaign against the Government's precautionary measures conducted by the native Press, and the expedient then adopted of strengthening the law against seditious publications merely served to intensify popular feeling. It was not till after 1898 that the Indian Government, recognizing the genuineness and sincerity of the public opposition to plague-restrictions, abandoned their more stringent rules in favour of milder methods.

In one direction only—the annual pilgrimage to the Hedjaz—may the plague be said to have brought any relief to the overworked police-force. The arrangements made by Messrs. Thomas Cook and Sons for shipping the pilgrims were discontinued about 1892, and in 1893 the Police Commissioner, acting through his pilgrim department and with the aid of the divisional and harbour police, shepherded the large number of 13,500 pilgrims to the embarkation sheds. Approximately the same number sailed in 1895. Directly the plague, however, had firmly established its hold upon Bombay, the annual exodus of pilgrims was prohibited, in response partly to international requirements, and during the remainder of Mr. Vincent's term of office the Haj traffic practically ceased. A few pilgrims from Central Asia (1300 in 1898) and other distant regions found their way yearly to Bombay, in the hope of proceeding to Mecca: but they were sent back every year to their homes, until the restrictions were removed and the traffic was re-opened.

Upon the health of the police force the plague naturally exercised a disastrous effect. A fairly high percentage of sickness was recorded in 1895 and was ascribed chiefly to overcrowding in squalid tenements. The appearance of plague in the last quarter of 1896 raised the death-roll of that year to 50 and increased the number of admissions to hospital by nearly 300. The experience of 1897 was worse. Eighty-two men died, of whom fifty-two were plague-victims : recruiting for the force entirely ceased. More than 3,000 admissions to hospital were recorded, some of the constables being obliged to undergo treatment there three or four times during the year. To make up in some degree for the deficit, the Commissioner was obliged to take men from the Ramoshi force, which supplies night-guards to shops and offices and is paid by the employers. Many of these semi-official watchmen also succumbed. Several years elapsed before the police-force recovered from the effects of the early years of the plague, when the loss of physical power of resistance to the disease, engendered by continuous overwork, was aggravated by the lack of commodious and sanitary lines and barracks. Those who, like the author, can recall the panic which prevailed in those years, and who day by day and night after night saw the sky above the Queen's road crimson with the glow of the funeral-pyres in the Hindu burning-ground, will not grudge a tribute of praise to the Indian constables who went about their work unflinchingly, while men were dying around them in hundreds and their own caste-fellows in the factories and the docks were flying from the scourge to their homes in the Deccan and the Konkan.

In 1893 occurred numerous strikes of mill-hands, which interfered to some extent with the ordinary work of the police and caused loss to the textile industry. But these outbreaks were trivial by comparison with the grave Hindu-Muhammadan riots, which broke out on August 11th in that year and afforded startling evidence of the deep sectarian antagonism which underlies the apparently calm surface of Indian social life and may at any moment burst forth in fury. The predisposing cause of the disturbance must be sought in the rioting which had occurred earlier in the year at Prabhas Patan in Kathiawar during the celebration of the Muharram, when a Muhammadan mob had destroyed temples and murdered several Hindus. For a fortnight or more before the outbreak of violence in Bombay, agitators had been at work among the more fanatical elements of the population and were assisted by leading Hindus, who convened large mass-meetings to denounce the authors of the outrages at Prabhas Patan. This agitation aroused intense irritation, which was aggravated by the persistent demand of the Hindus that the killing of cows, and even of sheep and goats, should be prohibited by Government. The Moslem population became fairly persuaded that the Hindus had the sympathy of the authorities and that their religion was in danger. They determined to rise *en masse* in its defence.

Shortly after midday on Friday, August 11th, a large Muhammadan congregation emerged from the Jama Masjid and amid cries of *Din, Din* ("the Faith") commenced to attack an important Hindu temple in Hanuman Lane. The more respectable Moslem worshippers took no part in this attempt to desecrate the temple and held aloof from all violence. But the low-class mob, which was constantly reinforced, took control of the neighbourhood for the time being. Mr. Vincent had foreseen the possibility of an attack upon the Hanuman Lane temple and had kept a large proportion of his force on duty up to 3 a. m. on Friday morning—a precaution which resulted in postponing the rising of the mob for a few hours. When the disturbance began, all but a small body of European and Indian police had been withdrawn for a much-needed rest, and it fell to the lot of these few men to hold the rioters in check, until the arrival of reinforcements drove the mob from the temple. Meanwhile the spirit of revenge spread rapidly, and within a short time the whole of Parel, Kamathipura, Grant road, Mazagon and Tank Bandar were given over to mob-law.

The tumult was enormous. The Muhammadans attacked every Hindu they met; the Hindus retaliated; and then both sides rounded on the police. Stones and *lathis* (iron-shod bamboo cudgels) were the rioters' chief weapons, and they were used with murderous effect. Little care was taken by the Muhammadans to confine their attacks to the enemies of the Faith. Peaceful wayfarers were brutally assaulted: tram-cars and carriages were murderously stoned; post-office vans were attacked; messengers carrying money were savagely beaten and openly robbed. The crowds, raging from street to street, demolished Hindu temples, and dragged out and desecrated the idols in the most obscene and shameful manner. The *Chilli-chors* or Musalman drivers of public conveyances, most of whom hail from the Palanpur State in Kathiawar, stormed the Hindu quarter of Kumbharwada, while the Julhais or Muhammadan weavers from upper India attacked the Pardeshi Hindu milk-merchants and set fire to the milch-cattle stables in Agripada. All business was perforce suspended and the whole city was thrown into the greatest consternation.

Noting the rapid spread of the disorder, Mr. Vincent applied early for military assistance with a view to restricting the area of rioting. At 4 p. m. two companies of the Marine Battalion under Colonel Shortland marched into the City and were followed in quick succession by the 10th Regiment N. I. under Colonel Forjett, son of Mr. Charles Forjett, by the Royal Lancashires under Colonel Ryley, and by a battery of Artillery. The Bombay Volunteer Artillery under Major Roughton and the Bombay Light Horse under Lieutenant Cuffe were also called out. The Government sent reinforcements of British and Indian troops from Poona, and detachments of armed police were also drafted into Bombay from Thana and other districts. The troops, which numbered three thousand with two guns, were under the orders of General Budgen. Eighteen European citizens were appointed Special Magistrates to assist the Presidency

Magistrates, Mr. Cooper and Mr. Webb, who were on duty in the streets night and day. The Municipal Commissioner, Mr. H. A. Acworth, and the Health Officer, Dr. Weir, made strenuous efforts to prevent the interruption of the sanitary service of the city, which in some wards temporarily broke down, and of the daily supply of food to the markets. One serious feature of the early part of the disturbance was the refusal of the butchers at Bandora to slaughter any cattle, and it needed prompt and tactful action on the part of Mr. Douglas Bennett, superintendent of municipal markets, to overcome their contumacy.

The troops were posted in various parts of the city and were forced to open fire on several occasions owing to the defiant attitude of the mob, which was being constantly reinforced. A notable instance occurred at the well-known Sulliman Chauki in Grant road, where a detachment of native infantry was so furiously attacked that it had to fire several times to avoid being overwhelmed by the rioters. Despite these measures, the rioting and looting continued on August 12th in all parts of the city, and many murders and assaults occurred also on the 13th. From the evening of the latter date, however, tranquillity gradually supervened, and eventually the efforts of the authorities, aided by the prominent men of both communities, effected a reconciliation between the excited belligerents.

The effects of the outbreak were for the time being serious. All business in the City was suspended for nearly ten days, and fifty thousand people, chiefly women and children, fled from Bombay to their homes up-country. About one hundred persons were killed, and nearly 800 were wounded, during the progress of the rioting, while the loss of property was enormous. The damage done to Hindu temples and Moslem mosques amounted respectively to Rs. 51,300 and Rs. 23,200, exclusive of the property stolen from them, which was estimated to be worth nearly 2 lakhs of rupees. During and for a few days after the disturbances, when the police were fully occupied in efforts to restore order and in prosecuting fifteen hundred persons arrested during the rioting, a great many cases of robbery, house-trespass and theft occurred, which, though registered by the police, could not be investigated and were never brought to court.

The second serious outbreak occurred in the last year of Mr. Vincent's term of office, and was due directly to the hostility of the public to the measures adopted by Government for combating the plague. The Julhais, or Jolahas, professional hand-weavers from the United Provinces, who have for many years formed a colony in the streets and lanes adjoining Ripon road, compose one of the most ignorant and fanatical sections of Muhammadans. The trouble commenced on March 9, 1898, with an attempt by a party of plague-searchers to remove a sufferer from a Julhai house in Ripon cross road. The Julhais in a body took alarm, seized their *lathis* and any weapon that came to hand, and attacked a body of police who had been sent to keep order and protect the plague-authorities. The position rapidly became serious; and as the mob refused to disperse and showed signs of increasing violence, the third Presidency Magistrate, Mr. P. H. Dastur, who had been summoned to the spot and had himself been slightly wounded by a stone, ordered the police to fire. This served for the moment to disperse the Julhai mob. But in a very short time the disorder spread to Bellasis, Duncan, Babula Tank, Grant, Parel, Falkland and Foras roads, where many Hindus were celebrating the last day of the annual Holi festival by idling and drinking. The rioters tried to set fire to the plague hospitals; murdered two English soldiers of the Shropshire Regiment in Grant road; burned down the gallows-screen near the jail; and tried to destroy the fire-brigade station in Babula Tank road. On this occasion also the Muhammadan butchers at the Bandora slaughter-house refused to do their work, but were eventually forced to remain on duty by Mr. Douglas Bennett, who hurried to Bandora with a small body of native infantry and taught the refractory a sound lesson. An unpleasant feature of the rioting was the attacks by the mob on isolated Europeans, several of whom were protected in the pluckiest manner by Indians of the lower classes. The outbreak was quickly quelled by military, naval and volunteer forces, who were wisely called out on the first sign of trouble. By the following day peace was restored. The casualties were officially stated to be 19 killed and 42 wounded, and the police arrested 247 persons for rioting, of whom 205 were convicted and sentenced to varying terms of imprisonment.

The Hindu-Muhammadan riots of 1893 were directly responsible for the establishment in Western India of the annual *public* celebrations in honour of the Hindu god Ganpati, which subsequently developed into one of the chief features of the anti-British revolutionary movement in India.[1] The riots left behind them a bitter legacy of sectarian rancour, which Bal Gangadhar Tilak utilized for broadening his new anti-British movement, by enlisting in its support the ancient Hindu antagonism to Islam. "He not only convoked popular meetings in which his fiery eloquence denounced the Muhammadans as the sworn foes of Hinduism, but he started an organization known as the "Anti-Cow-Killing Society," which was intended and regarded as a direct provocation to the Muhammadans, who, like ourselves, think it no sacrilege to eat beef." As his propaganda grew, assuming steadily a more anti-British character, Tilak decided to invest it with a definitely religious sanction, by placing it under the special patronage of the elephant-headed god Ganesh or Ganpati. In order to widen the breach between Hindus and Muhammadans, he and his co-agitators determined to organize annual festivals in honour of the god on the lines which had become familiar in the

1. The account which follows is taken, in some passages *verbatim*, from Sir V. Chirol's *Indian Unrest*, 1910.

Mr. S. M. EDWARDES

annual Muhammadan celebration of the Muharram. Their object was to make the procession, in which the god is borne to his final resting-place in the water, as offensive as possible to Moslem feelings by imitating closely the Muharram procession, when the *tazias* and *tabuts*, representing the tombs of the martyrs at Kerbela, are immersed in the river or sea.

Accordingly, on the approach of the Ganpati festival in September, 1894, Tilak and his party inaugurated a *Sarvajanik Ganpati* or public Ganpati celebration, providing for the worship of the god in places accessible to the public (it had till then been a domestic ceremony), and arranging that the images of Ganpati should have their *melas* or groups of attendants, like the Musalman *tolis* attending upon the *tabuts*. The members of these *melas* were trained in the art of fencing with sticks and other physical exercises. During the ten days of the festival, bands of young Hindus gave theatrical performances and sang religious songs, in which the legends of Hindu mythology were skilfully exploited to arouse hatred of the "foreigner," the word *mlenccha* or "foreigner" being applied equally to Europeans and Muhammadans. As the movement grew, leaflets were circulated, urging the Marathas to rebel as Shivaji did, and declaring that a religious outbreak should be the first step towards the overthrow of an alien power. As may be imagined, these Ganpati processions, which took place on the tenth day of the festival, were productive of much tumult and were well calculated to promote affrays with the Muhammadans and the police. A striking instance occurred in Poona, where a mela of 70 Hindus deliberately outraged Moslem sentiment by playing music and brawling outside a mosque during the hour of prayer.

These celebrations helped to intensify Tilak's seditious propaganda; and although they are barely mentioned in the annual reports of the Police Commissioner, they had become firmly established in Bombay and other places by the date of Mr. Vincent's retirement, and were destined to impose a heavy burden of extra work on the police-force for several years to come. At the present date the public celebration of the *Ganesh Chaturthi* still takes place and necessitates special traffic arrangements, when the crowds pour out of the city to immerse the clay-images of the god in Back Bay. But the more disturbing political features of the festival have gradually disappeared. This change may be held to date roughly from Tilak's second trial for sedition and conviction in 1908, which dealt a severe blow to the seditious side of the movement. A few *melas* appeared in the following years ; but the strength of the movement was broken by the incarceration of the leader of the Extremists and by judicious action on the part of the divisional and detective police.

This brief record of the period 1893 to 1898 will suffice to show that any improvement in the prevention and detection of crime, which might have been expected to follow on the increase in the numbers of the police force, was largely discounted by outbreaks of disorder and by the prevalence of a disastrous epidemic. With his police constantly being summoned to assist in plague-operations of a difficult character, and being forced in consequence of overwork and illness to seek constant treatment in hospital, the Commissioner was scarcely able to insist upon a standard of police-work suitable to normal times. In spite, however, of these difficulties and of additional work of a novel character arising out of the gradual spread of the anti-British revolutionary movement, the Bombay police under Mr. Vincent's control contrived to achieve reasonable success in their dealings with the criminal elements of the population, and set an example of adherence to duty under very trying conditions which earned more than once the express approbation of the Bombay Government.

Mr. HARTLEY KENNEDY

[Photograph taken 20 years after retirement]

CHAPTER VII

Mr. Hartley Kennedy, C.S.I.

1899—1901

When Mr. Vincent left India at the end of 1898, to spend the remainder of his days in Switzerland, he was succeeded by Mr. Hartley Kennedy of the Bombay District Police. Mr. Kennedy took charge of the Commissioner's office on January 9th, 1899. Like his predecessor, he had to reckon with the continued presence of plague, and also with the effect upon the urban police administration of severe famine in various districts of the Presidency. These natural disasters synchronized with a severe slump in the Bombay textile industry, due chiefly to over-production and the consequent glutting of the China market, which at that date absorbed the bulk of the Bombay mill-products. According to a leading mill-owner, the industry in 1899 was in a most critical position ; nearly all the mills were closed on three days in the week, and some had altogether ceased working. A strike of mill-hands was threatened, which the Police were called upon, and managed, to settle before it came to a head. The position of affairs in 1901 was very little better.

The police were thus faced with an abnormal volume of crime resulting from disease, starvation and unemployment. In 1899 two real dacoities of the type common in up-country districts, perpetrated probably by Pardesis from Northern India, occurred in the suburbs and obliged the Commissioner to establish night-patrols of mounted and foot police in the north of the Island. The following year witnessed a marked increase of crime against property, resulting from high prices and unemployment. Famine-conditions were responsible for an abnormal number of cases of exposure of infants in

1899 and for many instances of robbery by means of *dhatura* poisoning in 1900. But, apart from these temporary symptoms of economic disorder, the last decade of the nineteenth century witnessed a steady increase of cases of all kinds under the Indian Penal Code and miscellaneous laws. Cases under the Police Act would probably have shown a similar upward tendency, but for the fact that prosecutions were purposely avoided, in deference to the reluctance of the Presidency Magistrates to convict offenders on the sole evidence of police witnesses. It has always been difficult to find private persons willing to appear in court and give evidence in such matters.

As in most parts of India, the number of false complaints brought to the police was considerable, many of these cases falling within the category of "maliciously false". The Commissioner estimated the proportion of false to true cases in 1900 at one in 375. The false complaint, supported by false evidence, has been a feature of the criminal administration of India from early days and adequately explains the reason why Europeans have always clung so strenuously to the right, secured to them by the criminal law, of being tried by a jury containing a majority of their own countrymen. It is the only safeguard they possess against false prosecution and illegal conviction. Some such protection for the European minority is essential in a country, where the administration of justice by Indian courts has not reached so high and detached a level as it has in England.

The year 1901 was prolific of murders, twenty-one cases being investigated by the police. Among the chief *causes célèbres* was the murder in the streets by followers of H.H. the Aga Khan of certain Khojas belonging to the Asna Ashariya section, which had announced its determination to secede from the main body of Khojas. The precise reason for the murders is unknown. They may have been decided upon by one of the factions as a protest against the constant absences of H. H. the Aga Khan, or on the other hand may have been intended by the party which supported His Highness as a celebration of his safe return from abroad. Faction feeling in the community was at the time running high, and the more fanatical of the Aga Khan's followers were incensed with those Khojas who were disinclined to subscribe blindly to the opinions on communal matters held by the more conservative section. His Highness himself, who happened to be in Europe on one of his periodical visits, had no knowledge whatever of the murder-plot; otherwise his influence would certainly have been directed towards restraining the fury of his Ismailia followers. He himself was much perturbed by the tragedy and gave Mr. Kennedy every assistance in the enquiry which followed. The three victims were stabbed to death in the streets, almost at the moment of his arrival, and the police found their time fully occupied in trying to calm the passions thus aroused. The murders produced such rancour between the Ismailia and the Asna Ashariya Khojas that, for many years afterwards, the police were obliged to prohibit the funerals of the latter passing through the recognized Khoja quarters to their separate grave-yard in Mazagon. It was not until 1913 that the Commissioner found himself justified in relaxing the more stringent precautions, owing to the passage of time and the prevalence of a better feeling between the two sections of Khojas. The knives, with which the murders were committed, were preserved for many years in one of the lockers in the inner room of the Commissioner's office, and were handed over to the Criminal Investigation Department as an exhibit for the museum, when that branch was reorganized in 1910.

Most of the crime in respect of property was, as usual, committed by Mhar and Mang robbers from the Deccan, by the Wagris or gipsy tribes, by professional thieves and beggars from Kathiawar, and by north-country

Hindus and Pathans. Bombay has a large floating population of these wanderers, who visit the city for criminal purposes, and, having attained their object, travel to other parts of India, where all trace of them is frequently lost. Among cases of special importance were the prosecutions of two licensed dealers in arms and ammunition in 1899, a "golden gang" or swindling case in which a respectable Indian firm was cheated of Rs. 63,000, and which was successfully investigated by Inspector (afterwards Superintendent) Sloane, and the conviction for sedition of the editor of a vernacular newspaper, the *Gurakhi*, which, as an organ of the revolutionary party in Western India, had indulged in violent anti-British propaganda. The effect of plague and famine conditions upon the activities of the police was apparent in the returns of recovery of stolen property; and their normal duty of watch and ward suffered also to some extent from the imposition of such emergent tasks as the registration, accommodation, feeding and repatriation of a large number of war-refugees who arrived from the Transvaal in 1899. The restrictions upon the Haj traffic continued; but this did not absolve the police from the task of "shepherding" large numbers of returning pilgrims—the backwash of former pilgrimages—or of repatriating hundreds of poor and illiterate Moslems, who, knowing nothing of the stoppage of the traffic, arrived every year in Bombay in the hope of being allowed to embark for Jeddah.

The total strength of the police-force remained unaltered during Mr. Kennedy's term of office. Including the constables attached to the Veterinary Department, the force numbered 2118. The annual cost, however, had increased in 1900 to Rs. 792,959, in consequence of extra allowances and contingencies. These charges were met partly from imperial, partly from provincial, and partly from municipal and other revenues. The municipal contribution was recovered under section 62 of Bombay Act III of 1888, and continued to be so till 1907, when under the provisions of Bombay Act III of that year the Government became responsible for the whole cost of the force. Besides the police-force proper, the Commissioner recruited and controlled a force of 1048 Ramoshis or night-watchmen, whose wages, as previously mentioned, were recovered from the individuals and firms employing their services. The Ramoshis as a class were not very satisfactory; and though nominally under the supervision of the police-officers of the division or section in which their post lay, there was really no one to see whether they kept awake at night and really did their duty. Had there been any proper and comprehensive beat-system for the divisional constabulary, such as there is in London, the existence of a Ramoshi force would have been quite unnecessary: but the total number of police-constables was never sufficient to admit of the introduction of such a system.

For administrative purposes, Bombay was composed in 1899 of the eleven police divisions mentioned below, which were sub-divided into sections or areas controlled by a "police-station". The staff of a station comprised usually an European inspector and sub-inspector and a number of subordinate native officers (jemadar, havildar, naik) and constables.

Division	Sections
A	Fort
B	Umarkhadi, Market, Mandvi
C	Bhuleshwar, Nal Bazar, Dhobi Talao
D	Girgaum, Khetwadi, Mahalakshmi and Walkeshwar.
E	Byculla, Mazagon, Kamathipura
F	Dadar, Sewri, Matunga, Parel
G	Worli, Mahim
H and I	Harbour and Docks
K	Detective Branch
L	Reserve (Armed and unarmed)

Housing-accommodation was provided for only about one-tenth of the force. The Head Police Office at Crawford Market, which Colonel Wilson had so often asked for, was completed and occupied in 1899, and lines for 120 men had been built on the western boundary of the parade-ground adjacent to the Gokuldas Tejpal hospital. Stabling for twenty horses of the mounted police was also built, the main body of the mounted police being accommodated in the old Government House Bodyguard lines at Byculla. With the exception of the 200 men or so, who occupied the old police-lines in Byculla and the newly-erected quarters in the compound of the Head Police Office, the whole force was living in hired rooms of an undesirable and insanitary type in various parts of the city. The monthly house-allowance paid to constables barely sufficed to pay the rents of their squalid rooms, while in the case of the European officers it was quite insufficient to secure proper accommodation. The difficulty was acute in the A. division (Fort and Colaba), where suitable residential accommodation was extremely limited and fetched a high rent. To anyone, like the author of this book, who has seen the very unsuitable quarters in which most of the European and Indian police were obliged to reside at the beginning of the present century, it will always be a matter of surprise that the force accomplished as much as it did and that the death-roll among both Europeans and Indians was not far heavier. Even the comparatively modern buildings at Bazar Gate and Paidhoni left much to be desired in the way of reasonable space and ordinary comfort. The occupants of the Paidhoni station, which mounts guard over a crowded lower-class neighbourhood, possessed the additional disadvantage of an atmosphere heavy with the smells and miasmata of an Eastern city. It says much for the *dura ilia* of the British soldiers recruited for the Bombay police force that so many of them were able to live and carry on their work in these conditions without a permanent loss of health.

The reiterated complaints of successive Commissioners had impressed upon the Bombay Government the need for the proper housing of the force. But their wishes were dependent upon the state of the provincial exchequer, which after several years of plague and a series of disastrous famines was quite unable to provide money for police-accommodation schemes. A solution of the difficulty was, however, secured by the passing of Act IV of 1898 (City Improvement Trust Act), under the provisions of which the newly-constituted Trust could be called upon by the Government to build quarters and barracks for the police in various parts of the Island. By 1901 the Government had already formulated their first demands, and the engineers of the Trust were preparing plans and schemes for police stations, quarters and lines, in Colaba, Princess Street (a new street-scheme of the Trust), Nagpada and Agripada and in other crowded localities. These buildings took many years to complete, and some of them in the northern suburbs had not been commenced in 1916. But the first step towards a comprehensive solution of the grave problem of police-accommodation was taken during Mr. Kennedy's *régime*, when the City Improvement Trust assumed the task which the Government with the best will in the world, found themselves quite unable to fulfil.

Though his period of office was not long, Mr. Kennedy left his mark upon the police administration, and there are persons still alive who remember the energy and activity with which he tackled some of the evils of urban life. He was a sworn foe of gambling in any form, and had barely gripped the reins of office ere he commenced an offensive against the bagatelle-players, the cardsharpers and the dice-gamblers of the lower quarters. The divisional police learned to their cost that it did not pay to wink at gaming, and that the Commissioner, working through private agents of his own, possessed an uncomfortably accurate knowledge of what was going on in various quarters of the city. The performances of one of his chief informers are still within the recollection of the oldest members of the force and of some of the superannuated gamblers of the old B. and C. divisions. The immediate result of Mr. Kennedy's action was a large increase of cases under the Gambling Act, sixty prosecutions being launched in the year 1900 alone. The effect of these prosecutions, however, was minimised by the Magistrates' practice of imposing merely a fine on conviction. Such fines acted as very little deterrent to men who dealt week by week with comparatively large sums of money. In the case of the most inveterate gamblers a short term of imprisonment would probably have had a more salutary effect.

Another problem, which occupied Mr. Kennedy's attention, was that of the beggars who infest Bombay. They comprised not only the thousands of able-bodied religious mendicants, who form an integral feature of Hinduism and are largely protected from official action by the religious atmosphere surrounding them, but also the still larger class of professional beggars of every sect, who descend on the city like locusts from the rural districts and do not hesitate, as opportunity occurs, to commit crime. In 1899 Mr. Kennedy raised the question of the best method of dealing with the latter class, and pointed out that daily prosecution, followed by the imposition of a small fine, failed entirely to effect any amelioration of the evil. He therefore decided on more drastic measures. In 1900 he deported 9,000 beggars to the territories of Indian Princes and 10,000 to various districts in British India. This wholesale expulsion caused a temporary improvement in the condition of the streets. But such deportations, to be really effective, must be carried on ruthlessly year by year; and methods would have to be adopted to penalise beggars of an undesirable type, who dared to return after deportation. Mr. Kennedy's action was not pursued by his successors, and the beggar-nuisance consequently continued unabated. In 1920 it had become so intolerable that a special committee of Government and Municipal representatives was appointed to study the problem in all its bearings and devise measures for its solution.

In the matter of the immoral traffic in women Mr. Kennedy displayed equal activity and achieved more success. The foreign pimp and procurer, who swooped down at intervals upon Bombay to acquaint himself with the demand for fresh women and to relieve the European prostitutes of their earnings, met with no mercy at his hands. He used the provisions of the Aliens Act freely against them, deporting 30 of them in 1900 and 37 in 1901. Officers of the detective branch were entrusted specially with the duty of watching the European brothels, meeting the steamers of foreign shipping-companies, and marking down every Jewish trafficker who showed his nose in Bombay. It is only quite recently that the Indian Government, in response to domestic and international opinion, have strengthened the provisions of the Foreigners Act, in order to give the police in Bombay and other large maritime cities more effective control over these disreputable and degraded persons: and as a result of the pressure of public opinion, endorsed by the League of Nations, the activities of the international trafficker are more restricted and more easily controlled than they were at the close of the nineteenth century. It is much to Mr. Kennedy's credit that, working with the unamended Act, he was able in two years to secure a definite reduction in the number of professional traffickers visiting Bombay.

He paid constant attention also to the offence of kidnapping or procuring minor Indian girls for immoral purposes. It is well known that both Hindu and Muhammadan recruits for the prostitutes' profession are obtained from among the illegitimate children of courtesans, or from among female children adopted by prostitutes, or thirdly, by purchase from agents who travel throughout

Gujarat, Central India, Rajputana and other districts, picking up superfluous and unwanted girls of tender age for a small sum, sometimes as little as Rs. 5 or Rs. 6, and then selling them at a profit to brothel-keepers in the large cities and towns. Leaving out of consideration the custom, prevalent among Maratha Kunbis and Mhars, of dedicating their female children to the god Khandoba, which in practice condemns the girls to a life of prostitution, and the customs of degraded nomadic tribes like the Kolhatis, Dombars, Harnis, Berads and Mang Garudas, who habitually prostitute their girls, it may be said that among the lower social strata in India female life is held very cheap. A daughter is apt to be regarded rather as a domestic calamity, owing largely to the heavy expense usually involved in getting her married. Cases therefore often occur of young girls being abandoned by their relatives, who are unable to provide the funds required for their regular betrothal; and these little derelicts sometimes drift into brothels, where they are fed, clothed and taught singing and dancing until they reach puberty, when the brothel-keeper arranges to sell their first favours for a round sum to some well-to-do libertine. Muhammadan prostitutes, who are numerous throughout India and range from the inmate of the low-class brothel to the wealthy courtesan, who earns a high fee for her singing, occupies well-furnished quarters, and drives in her own motor-car or carriage, are recruited in the same way. In one case, which occurred a few years ago, a lower class Moplah of the Malabar coast, having borrowed money at a high rate of interest to provide dowries for his two elder daughters and being unable to raise any further sum for his third daughter's betrothal, sold her outright to a Bombay brothel-keeper for Rs. 40. The girl was about eight years of age when she entered the brothel, and by the age of thirteen she was helping to support her worthless father and two young brothers out of her earnings as a prostitute.

Mr. Kennedy also pointed out to Government that year by year "scores of young girls," belonging chiefly to

Gujarat and Kathiawar, were either picked off the streets by native pimps of both sexes or were, as mentioned above, brought down from rural areas by regular traffickers and sold to the local brothel-keepers for sums ranging from Rs. 10 to Rs. 50. In many cases the police rescued these waifs and restored them to their homes: but they could not make much headway against a system which had attained such large proportions. Moreover, in addition to the difficulty of tracing the girls' relatives in a country like India, their task was not rendered easier by the absence of any strong public opinion against such practices, and by the non-existence of properly organized orphanages and homes. In several instances girls were discovered prostituting themselves under compulsion from a male "bully" or female brothel-keeper; and in such cases, as well as in cases of kidnapping, every effort was made by the police, under Mr. Kennedy's orders, to arrest the offenders and bring them to trial. Wherever it was impossible to secure the conviction of an offender under the Indian Penal Code, Mr. Kennedy had resort to the provisions of Chapter VIII of the Criminal Procedure Code. Here he met with more success than his predecessor, who, as already mentioned, complained that the Magistrates required evidence under that chapter which it was extremely difficult to procure. Mr. Kennedy found in Chapter VIII, C. P. C. an invaluable weapon against "bullies" and other bad characters of the same type, whom it was inexpedient or impossible to charge with an offence under the Penal Code; and the Magistrates showed no objection whatever to supporting the action of the police in such cases. Thus for three years a very wholesome check was placed upon this deplorable traffic, at a time when there was little articulate Indian opinion to support the activity of the Commissioner. It was not till twelve or thirteen years later that the Indian Government was invited to consider Bills introduced by non-official Indian members of the Legislature, designed to check or suppress both the immigration of European unfortunates and the *swadeshi* traffic in minor Indian girls.

Mr. Kennedy's personal activities during the earlier months of his Commissionership were to some extent reminiscent of the methods of Mr. Forjett. He is said to have sometimes assumed a disguise—the full-dress of an Arab or the *burka* or covering of a Musalman *pardah-nashin*,—and thus attired to have wandered about the city after nightfall in company with one of his agents. He would pay surprise visits in this way to various police-stations and *chaukis*, in order to discover at first hand what sort of work his European and native officers were doing; and all ranks learned to fear the consequences of their negligence or other shortcomings being discovered by the Commissioner and performed their duties with greater caution and zeal. He made himself feared by the evil-doer and the lazy, who tried occasionally to forestall him by obtaining previous information of his nocturnal visitations. They met, however, with little success; the Commissioner was more than a match for them. These constant surprise visits during 1899 and 1900 enabled him to keep his finger on the pulse of the city and to checkmate the criminal on several occasions. During the greater part of his term of office, however, an injury to one of his ankles, which produced a limp, practically deprived him of the power to pass unnoticed in disguise. The lower classes thenceforth knew him as *Langada Kandi Saheb*, i. e. 'the lame Mr. Kennedy', and he is thus spoken of to this day by the old law-breakers and disreputables who recollect his efforts to bring them to book.

Short as was his tenure of the Commissioner's appointment, Mr. Kennedy managed to inspire the unworthy, whether belonging to the police-force or to the lower-class urban population, with a wholesome fear of retribution; and he spared no effort to tighten up the divisional police administration, to discover by personal inquiry the character of his subordinates, and to place a check upon immorality. The discipline which he inculcated in the police force was evident at the census of 1901, when, in response to the request of the census authorities for assistance in enumerating the large cosmopolitan population of the city, he placed his European police officers in chargé of the census-sections, directed the Sirdar Mir Abdul Ali to secure the co-operation of the leaders of the various sections and castes among the lower classes, and made the divisional police responsible on the actual night of the census for counting the large army of homeless and wandering people, who are a permanent feature of the capital of Western India. Mr. Lovat Fraser, then editor of the *Times of India,* wrote a graphic account in his paper of this "Counting by Candle-light", and paid a tribute to the thoroughness of the census organization. The author of this book, who happened to be in charge of the urban census, under the orders of the Provincial Superintendent, Mr. R. E. Enthoven, can testify truly that his plans for the enumeration could not have been successful without the active assistance of a police-force inspired by its chief with a high standard of efficiency.

CHAPTER VIII

MR. H. G. GELL, M.V.O.

1902—1909

When Mr. Kennedy left Bombay on furlough preparatory to retirement, his place was taken by Mr. Herbert G. Gell, who had held the substantive appointment of Deputy Commissioner since 1884, and on three occasions had acted for short periods as Commissioner. "Jel Saheb," as the Indian constables called him, was thus no stranger to the police-force or to Bombay, when he took charge of the Commissioner's office. So far as personal popularity with all classes was concerned, the Government could not have made a happier selection. In his younger days Mr. Gell had been a good cricketer and the best racket-player in Bombay; and while this counted in his favour chiefly with his own countrymen, his genial address and straight-forwardness commended themselves equally to Europeans and Indians. During his term of office, which lasted a little more than seven years, he was granted furlough twice—in 1904 when Mr. Michael Kennedy, afterwards Inspector-General of Police, Bombay Presidency, carried on his duties, and again in 1906 when Mr. W. L. B. Souter, a son of Sir Frank Souter, acted as *locum tenens*. During Mr. Gell's first year of office, the Deputy Commissioner's post was filled by Superintendent J. Crummy, a good police officer of the old type, who joined the force as a constable in 1866 and finally retired from the service in 1903. He was succeeded by Mr. R. P. Lambert (1903–1905), Mr. Reinold, who died prematurely, and Mr. R. M. Phillips (1905–09), all of whom belonged to the Imperial Indian Police service.

The years of Mr. Gell's administration were fraught with anxiety and difficulties of various kinds. Social and semi-political events like the festivities in connexion with

Mr. H. G. GELL

the Coronation of King Edward VII and the visit of the Duke and Duchess of Connaught in 1903, the arrival of the Prince and Princess of Wales in 1905, and the visit of the Amir Habibullah of Afghanistan in 1907, imposed much extra work upon the force. On the whole, however, they probably caused the Commissioner less real anxiety than the Muharram riots of 1904, the Bombay Postal strike of 1906, the mill-hand strikes of 1907 and 1908, the serious Tilak riots of 1908, and last but not least the strike of the Bombay Indian constabulary in 1907. Besides these symptoms of local discontent, the Commissioner and his somewhat old-fashioned detective agency had to grapple with a constantly growing stream of enquiries, reports and references, arising out of the spread of the dangerous Indian revolutionary movement, which was partly fostered and directed by men of extreme views living in France and America.

The baneful activities of Krishnavarma and the India House in London, of the brothers Savarkar, of Bal Gangadhar Tilak in the Deccan, and of the anarchists of Bengal, had many ramifications in India, and, coupled with the malignant incitements to sedition disseminated by certain vernacular newspapers, imposed a large burden of confidential and secret work upon the various provincial and urban police-forces. Some of these were but poorly equipped to cope with this secret menace to the State. Bombay from its proximity to the Deccan, which was the focus of intrigue in western India, and from its position as the chief port of arrival from Europe, had an important part to play in the official struggle against the revolutionary movement. The difficulties which beset Mr. Gell's administration resulted largely from the fact that he was working with a machine designed for dealing mainly with ordinary urban crime against person and property, and numerically inadequate even for that purpose. A thorough reorganization in respect of personnel, numbers and pay was required to render the Bombay police force capable of dealing effectively with the problems of the early years of the twentieth century.

The total numbers of the force in 1902 were 2,126 and the annual cost Rs. 773,580. The numbers remained practically stationary during Mr. Gell's *régime*, despite a great expansion of the residential area and a steady increase of population during the first decade of the present century. The prolonged visitation of the plague led many of the richer Indian merchants to forsake their old family-houses in the crowded and low-lying parts of the city and to seek a new domicile on Malabar and Cumballa hills, which had previously been occupied almost wholly by European residents. Many of the less well-to-do citizens sought new quarters in the empty areas (the F and G divisions) in the north of the Island. The Commissioner drew the attention of Government in 1903 to the alterations which were taking place in Mahim, Sion, Matunga, Naigaon and adjacent parts, and emphasized the consequent need of more police for watch and ward. His view was corroborated by the census taken by the Muncipal Health authorities in 1906, which showed that the total population of Bombay had increased by more than 200,000 since 1901, the increase being general over all sections of the City and Island. In the light of these facts a revision of the police establishment was obviously necessary, and but for two events of primary importance it would probably have taken the form of spasmodic increments to the existing strength and small enhancements in the salaries and allowances of the constabulary.

The first important event was the publication in 1905 of the report of the Police Commission appointed by Lord Curzon and presided over by Sir Andrew Frazer. Of the Indian police service generally the report was highly condemnatory, declaring it to be 'far from efficient...... defective in training and organization......inadequately supervised...........and generally regarded as corrupt and oppressive.' Though these strictures referred chiefly to the district police forces of the various provinces, it was admitted that the police organization of the large cities required considerable overhauling. The Commissioners of Police in Calcutta, Bombay and Madras were therefore instructed to submit proposals for a thorough reorganization, based *mutatis mutandis* upon the broad lines laid down by the Police Commission. Owing to pressure of work and other reasons Mr. Gell did not submit his proposals for reform for more than two years after the publication of the report of Sir A. Frazer's Commission, and when they eventually reached the Bombay Government, the latter found it impossible to accept them. Moreover, circumstances connected with the outbreak and handling of the Tilak riots of July, 1908, led Government to believe that the police force needed a far more comprehensive reorganization than was contemplated by the Commissioner.

In September, 1908, therefore, the Governor, Sir George Clarke, (afterwards Lord Sydenham) appointed a special committee of three officials—Mr. (afterwards Sir William) Morison of the Indian Civil Service, Mr. S. M. Edwardes, also a member of the I. C. S., and Mr. Pheroze H. Dastur, 2nd Presidency Magistrate—to scrutinize Mr. Gell's proposals, to take any evidence that might seem necessary, and finally to submit detailed proposals for the numerical strength, pay and duties of the various branches of the Police force. This committee held several meetings in September and October, examined the Commissioner, Deputy Commissioner and other members of the force, as well as certain leading citizens, and submitted its report at the end of October, 1908. The policy and proposals therein advocated met with the approval of the Bombay Government; but the further step of introducing the changes in the constitution of the force thereby involved, was not undertaken until after Mr. Gell's departure on leave in 1909. The broad details of the scheme eventually sanctioned in September, 1910, can be explained more suitably in the next chapter, which deals with the administration of Mr. Gell's successor. The facts mentioned above show the reason why the actual numbers of the force at the date of Mr. Gell's departure were practically the same as they had been in 1902.

The second event of importance was the police strike, which obliged the Bombay Government to introduce revised rates of pay for the constabulary in advance of the general reorganization of the force. Rents in the city and the cost of living had been steadily rising since 1900, and the Indian police-constables, in common with other low-paid servants of Government, found the burden of supporting themselves and their families almost intolerable. The majority of them were Konkani Marathas—the large class which supplies the bulk of the mill-labour and the menial staff in public and private offices, and they could not remain unaffected by the general demand for higher wages which was being made at this time to all employers of labour. Their superior officers had assured them more than once that their appeals were being favourably considered and that some concessions would be granted, while the open sympathy with their circumstances and their difficulties shown by Mr. Souter, when acting as Commissioner in 1906, inspired them with the idea that their claim to increased pay was absolutely unquestioned and deserved instant confirmation by Government. They were also affected to some extent by the constant and often bitter criticism of the authorities, which appeared in the native Press, and by the incitements of professional agitators who urged them to follow the lead of the postmen, who went on strike in 1906, and adopt more overt measures to secure their demands. The unrest thus created culminated in a strike of a large proportion of the constabulary in 1907. Refusing to don their uniforms and report themselves for duty until Government assented to their request for higher pay, the men assembled in a body on the Esplanade *maidan*, where they were addressed by the chief agitators in their own ranks. The Commissioner was left to carry out the routine-work of the force with the help of the European police, a certain number of constables who remained loyal, and the comparatively useless body of Ramoshis. In brief, the police administration was practically at a standstill.

By resorting to a strike, the men had rendered themselves individually liable to prosecution; and when the strike was declared, Mr. Gell, with the approval of Government, caused some of the ring-leaders to be arrested. But the Bombay Government was aware that their resort to illegitimate action was the outcome of a real grievance, which could only be redressed by enhancing the pay of the various grades. Consequently, of the men arrested, only two were subsequently placed before the Courts and sentenced to pay a nominal fine; and they and others were afterwards reinstated in the force. Simultaneously the Government sanctioned the long-delayed increase in the pay of the constables and native officers. The old fourth-grade constable on Rs. 10 per mensem disappeared for ever, the monthly pay of the lowest rank being fixed at Rs. 12 and of the three upper ranks at Rs. 13, Rs. 14, and Rs. 15. The pay of the havildars was also augmented. The announcement of the new rates put an end to the *impasse* caused by the men's defection, and within a few days the force was again working with full vigour.

It was unfortunate that the concessions in respect of pay and allowances should have had the appearance of being extorted from the authorities by methods which, often objectionable in the case of private employees, are deplorable in the case of men appointed to be guardians of the public peace. The Bombay Government was not so much to blame for procrastination as might at first appear. They were perfectly prepared to grant the required increments of salary to the lower ranks of the force: but they wished to treat the revision of salaries as part and parcel of the general reorganization, rendered necessary by the Report of the Police Commission and by the increase of work resulting from the growth of the

City. They had instructed the Commissioner to formulate proposals for reorganization, which had not been submitted at the date of the strike, and which, when they eventually received them in 1908, they found themselves unable to approve without further enquiry by an independent committee. The responsibility for the delay in granting relief to the constabulary cannot therefore be assigned wholly to the Bombay Government. A more rapid effort to prepare without delay a comprehensive scheme of reform might have helped to prevent the occurrence of an episode, which did not redound to the credit of the force.

The result of the revision of the pay of native officers and constables, secured in the manner described above, was an increase of the annual cost of the force from Rs. 773,000 odd in 1902 to Rs. 975,000 in 1908. These charges fell wholly upon the Provincial Government, in accordance with the provisions of the Bombay Police Charges Act of 1907. Since 1872 the cost of the force had been borne partly by Government and partly by the Bombay Municipality under Act III of 1872 and the subsequent Act III of 1888. The arrangement did not prove wholly satisfactory, and the Municipal Corporation evinced a tendency to deprecate increased expenditure on a department over which it had no direct control. After much discussion, therefore, between the Bombay Government and the Corporation's representatives, Bombay Act III of 1907 was passed by the legislature. Under this enactment the Government was pledged to pay the whole charges of the police-force, and the Municipal Corporation was bound in return to shoulder the cost of primary education and, within certain limits, the cost of medical relief in the City. This arrangement in no wise absolved the Bombay Port Trust from its liability to pay a moiety of the charges of the harbour police and the entire cost of the police employed in the docks. On the other hand it enabled the Government to sanction, without the intervention or concurrence of the Corporation, such additional expenditure as might be involved in a thorough scheme of reorganization. When the latter scheme had been introduced by Mr. Gell's successor, the improvement and standardization of the uniform of the European officers of the force and the abolition of the old municipal helmet-badges followed naturally upon the settlement of the changes embodied in the Act.

Another important matter in the legislative sphere was the passing of the Bombay City Police Act IV of 1902, which consolidated the provisions of the preceding enactments and vested the whole control of the police force in the Commissioner. The Act removed the difficulties of which Mr. Kennedy had complained in 1898, and furnished the police with all the legal authority required for the performance of watch and ward duties, the investigation of offences, and the arrest and detention of wrong-doers.

During the first decade of the twentieth century the volume of crime steadily increased. The annual average number of cases for the quinquennial periods ending in 1900 and 1905 was respectively 32,411 and 30,814 : in 1908 the police dealt with nearly 41,000 cases. The number of persons arrested likewise increased from 37,000 in 1900 to 44,000 in 1908, while the number of convictions secured in 1908 was 41,500, as compared with 19,900 in 1880 and 34,450 in 1900. The value of property stolen in 1880 was estimated at Rs. 146,000; in 1900 at Rs. 333,000; and in 1908 at Rs. 353,000; while the percentage of recoveries during Mr. Gell's *régime* decreased from 59 in 1902 to 37 in 1905 and rose again to 56 in 1908. The annual migration of the people to plague-camps during the hot months still offered special facilities to the professional housebreaker, and was occasionally responsible, as in 1903, for an abnormal number of thefts. A somewhat similar epidemic of robberies resulted from the immigration of famine-stricken refugees in 1906. Many of these cases defied investigation, as they were not immediately reported; and in the case of thefts from houses temporarily vacated during the season of heavy plague-mortality, the losses were often not reported to the police until the owners returned two or three months afterwards to their homes.

These failures, which may be ascribed in some measure to the absence of a proper beat-system, were counter-balanced by the capture of two notorious professional house-breakers, one of whom was a Parsi, Nanabhai Dinshaw Daruwala, and the other a Borah named Tyebali Alibhai. Nanabhai was a criminal of more than ordinary courage and address, who had gathered around him a gang of clever assistants and had contrived to defy justice for more than twenty years. He had amassed considerable wealth by his house-breaking exploits, and as he spent his ill-gotten gains freely and was ready to pay ample hush-money, he secured immunity from arrest for many years. His capture was long sought without success. But at last, in 1907, the detective police managed to run him to ground, and, despite the offer of heavy bribes for his release, secured his conviction and imprisonment for a long term of years. The Borah, Tyebali, was a man of much less abiltity, and confined his attention almost entirely to the houses of respectable residents on Malabar Hill. In this area he carried out a series of daring robberies both by day and night, and had disposed of much valuable plate and jewellery before he was finally arrested and convicted in 1908.

Hardly a year passed without one or more murders, the number which occurred in 1902 and 1904 being respectively 18 and 20. Most of them were of the usual type—murder for the purpose of robbery or as the punishment of a wife or mistress for infidelity. With a few exceptions, all these cases were successfully investigated by the detective branch of the force. A prolonged and complicated series of forgeries, devised and carried out by eighteen men possessed of education and private means, was cleverly brought home to the culprits by Superintendent Sloane, who was appointed head of the detective branch on the retirement of the Sirdar Mir Abdul Ali in 1903.[1]

Neither the divisional nor the detective police, however, succeeded in discovering the origin of the disastrous cotton-fires which took place at Colaba in 1906. The value of the cotton destroyed or rendered unsaleable was estimated at 40 lakhs of rupees. Since that date similar conflagrations have occurred at intervals, in circumstances which seem to justify more than a suspicion of deliberate incendiarism. But in spite of special precautions and special police arrangements no practical proof of complicity has ever been obtained. In 1913 these fires at the Colaba cotton-green were so frequent and so disastrous that the Bombay Government appointed a special committee under the chairmanship of Mr. S. M. Edwardes, the Commissioner of Police at that date, to investigate the circumstances and origin of the conflagrations and make proposals for minimising the risk of them in future. The result of that committee's enquiry will be mentioned on a later page; but it may be here stated that on each occasion of these wholesale conflagrations at the old Colaba cotton-green the police found it very difficult to initiate and prosecute inquiries about firms or individuals, suspected of aiding and abetting incendiarism, owing to the disinclination of the insurance companies, with whom the cotton was insured, to assist the inquiries or register a formal complaint in respect of their losses. The system of underwriting adopted by all the fire insurance companies in Bombay resulted in the net loss incurred in any fire being divided among so many parties that the actual sum paid out by the company concerned was comparatively trivial, and

1. The Sirdar served for 38 years, having joined the force as a second-class Jemadar in 1865. Apart from his work as a detective, he is remembered as the founder of the Maratha Plague Hospital, which he organised and opened in 1898.

did not, in their view, justify the adoption of proceedings, which might have frightened the cotton-merchants into refusing to insure their goods with them in future. Consequently, the only chance the police had of discovering an offence was to arrest an incendiary *in flagrante delicto*, and this was rendered practically impossible by the character of the cotton, which will smoulder unseen for some time before it bursts into flame, by the enormous width and height of the stacks of cotton-bales, crowded on far too small an area on the edge of a main thoroughfare, and by the ease with which any person could escape detection in the labyrinth formed by the various *jethas* or collections of bales.

The question of traffic regulation in the streets demanded attention during this period. By 1903 the number of public and private conveyances in Bombay had risen to nearly 16,000, and although the style and condition of the victorias plying for hire showed considerable improvement,[1] rash driving was exceedingly common and street accidents had largely increased. The position was aggravated by a steady rise in the number of motor-vehicles, necessitating the creation of a special branch of the police-force for the registration of motor-cars and the issue of driving-licenses. One of the first owners of a car in Bombay during the closing years of the nineteenth century was the late Mr. B. H. Hewitt, one of the Municipal Engineers; and after 1900 his example was followed by a constantly increasing number of residents, some of whom showed a tendency to drive at excessive speed and to pay little attention to the orders of the police on traffic-duty. Thus, between 1905 and 1907 more than 900 new motor-cars appeared on the streets, and in the latter year the traffic-problem was further complicated by the abolition of the old horse-tramcars and the opening on May 7th of the electric tramways.

In these circumstances the incapacity of the average Indian constable to regulate traffic in the European

1. G. R. J. D. 3051 of June 4th, 1903.

manner became more marked, and some of the Divisional Superintendents had to spend more time than they could really spare in trying to inculcate an aptitude for directing and controlling pedestrian and wheeled traffic. Their efforts were not very successful, and it was generally felt that, although a few Indian officers and constables had profited by tuition and showed improvement in this branch of their duties, the presence of European police was absolutely essential at crowded points during the busy hours of the day. As previously remarked, the difficulties of the Indian constable were much aggravated by the studied disregard of his orders and warnings, frequently shown by his own compatriots.

As regards the beggar nuisance, Mr. Gell was disposed to continue the policy of his predecessor; and accordingly in 1902 he deported no less than 10,000 mendicants, mostly belonging to the territories of Indian Princes. But this procedure was peremptorily forbidden by Government in the following year, on the grounds that deportees of this class were prolific disseminators of plague infection. After 1903, therefore, the expulsion of beggars ceased, with the result that Bombay became once again a popular resort for penurious and homeless vagrants from all parts of India.

Efforts to rid Bombay of the foreign procurers, who subsisted on the traffic in European women, continued unabated. In 1909 the Commissioner deported 29 of these rascals; in 1903, 30; in 1904, 20; and in 1905, 2. No action was recorded in 1906 and 1907, but ten men were deported in 1908. These figures indicate in some measure the dimensions of the traffic and the lucrative nature of the business. The prospect of trivial profits would scarcely have persuaded 81 aliens within a period of four years to risk the chances of arrest and deportation. The history and description of these foreigners were recorded in the files of the detective branch, and in most cases their finger-print impressions were taken by the Criminal Identification Bureau, which under the auspices of Mr. Kirtikar and his assistant was rapidly acquiring a reputation for useful work.

The daily work of the police in the courts was directly affected by the establishment in 1904 of three benches of honorary magistrates in Girgaum, Mazagon and Dadar, which were intended to afford relief to the Chief Presidency Magistrate, Mr. J. Sanders Slater, and his three colleagues in the disposal of unimportant police cases. A fourth bench was established at the Esplanade Police Court in 1908, to deal with petty cases from the Harbour and Docks. These benches were empowered to deal with cases arising under certain sections of the Bombay City Police Act, the Prevention of Cruelty to Animals Act, the Public Conveyance Act, the Gambling Act, the Railways Act, and under section 352 of the Indian Penal Code. They proved very convenient to the police of the outlying F and G divisions, who were formerly obliged to bring offenders and witnesses all the way to the stipendiary court in Mazagon, but they involved much extra work for the European police officers of the various sections, who had frequently to attend both the stipendiary and honorary magistrates' courts. The latter commenced their work daily at 8-45 a. m., and the stipendiary courts at 11 a. m., so that European officers of busy sections had often to spend most of the working day in the courts. During their absence the registration and investigation of complaints at the police-station had perforce to remain in abeyance. One of the most urgent requirements during Mr. Gell's Commissionership was the creation of properly equipped and staffed police-stations, at which, no matter what the volume of work in the courts, at least one superior police officer would be found on duty at any hour of the day or night, ready to record complaints and initiate inquiries. The establishment of the benches of honorary magistrates served to accentuate the inadequacy of the old police system and the inability of

RAO SAHEB DAJI GANGAJI RANE

the force to cope with a greatly increased volume of case-work.

A serious obstacle to any re-arrangement of duties was the illiteracy of the great majority of the Indian subordinate officers and constabulary. As early as 1868 the Bombay Government asked the Commissioner to mention in his annual reports the progress made by the police in simple reading and writing; to which the Commissioner replied that as each member of the force was on actual duty for twelve hours out of the twenty-four, any form of education was impracticable. In 1885, when the total strength of the force was 1,721, there were only 113 officers and 362 men able to read and write, and of these only the European officers were literate in English. These numbers had slightly increased by the end of the following decade, in consequence presumably of the gradual spread of primary education. The numbers of officers and men able to read and write in 1896 were respectively 194 and 570. Occasionally an Indian with practically no education would rise to a high grade in the force by sheer natural ability and devotion to duty. Such men were the Subehdars Ramchandra and Daji and Inspector Khan Bahadur Sheik Ibrahim Imam, of whom the latter served for 47 years and on his retirement in 1911 was granted by the Bombay Government a special *jagir* (landed estate) in the Poona District, in recognition of his long and meritorious service.[1] The value of these men lay in their extraordinary knowledge of the urban population, their *flair* for criminal investigation, and their power of mediation between conflicting sects. Their lack of education and their ignorance of English debarred them from affording any relief to the European police in the registration of complaints and the prosecution of offenders in the courts.

1. He received the title of Khan Bahadur in 1904 and the King's Police Medal in 1910.

No effort had been made to open a career in the force for literate Indians of the upper-classes, and it became obvious during Mr. Gell's *régime* that in this respect the composition of the force had not kept abreast of the spirit of the age. While the general standard of literacy in Bombay had widened appreciably, and the growth of population had resulted in an increased number of cases of all kinds, the bulk of the Indian element in the force remained ignorant of English and was also often uneducated in its own vernaculars. Consequently the whole responsibility for the routine duties of the force fell upon a limited number of European officers, many of whom could claim no higher standard of education than that provided for the rank and file of the British Army. Among the latter, however, there were men of natural ability who by dint of application and study at odd moments had acquired a fair standard of general knowledge and could frame a good report of facts. To this category belonged men like Superintendents McDermott, Grennan, Nolan, Sloane, Williamson and others; and on their reports and administrative capacity the Commissioner and his Deputy necessarily placed much reliance. There were others, however, who acquired no literary polish throughout their career and whose educational attainments were no higher than when they first joined the force as supernumerary sub-inspectors. On the other hand, these men were always a solid asset in times of popular disturbance or at seasons of public festivity requiring the preservation of order among large crowds. From the Superintendent down to the latest joined Sub-Inspector, the European police contributed the leaven, which stiffened the force at the periodical Muharram outbreaks and ensured the orderly progress of events on the occasions of Royal and Vice-regal visits.

The annual pilgrimage to Mecca again assumed large proportions during these years. In 1902 the restrictions, imposed originally as a precautionary plague-measure, were abolished, and the period opened with the arrival in Bombay of about 1,000 pilgrims and with the return of 3,376 Hajis, who had to be repatriated to various districts of British India. In the following year the number of outgoing pilgrims was 8,700, and in 1904, 16,593, the large increase in the latter year being ascribable to the occurrence of the *Akbari Haj*, which falls once in ten years. But the traffic continued to expand. In 1905, 19,000 pilgrims embarked at Bombay for Jeddah and nearly 14,000 returned; in 1906, 24,300 embarked and 16,000 returned; and in 1907 more than 20,000 from all parts of India, from Bokhara, Turkestan and other parts of Central Asia, from Ceylon and Java, had to be shepherded on board by the Pilgrim Department of the Commissioner's office. The majority of these people were wholly uneducated; the existing *musafirkhanas* (rest-houses) provided for them in the City were quite inadequate for their proper accommodation; while the vessels provided for the passage to Jeddah by two or three merchants or companies were ill-found and equipped, and were becoming unseaworthy by reason of age.

At the same time the treatment of the pilgrims at various stages of their self-imposed journey, the behaviour of the pilgrim-brokers, who arranged for the purchase of tickets and were responsible generally for assisting pilgrims under the supervision of the Pilgrim Department, the arrangements for their embarkation and the disinfection of their clothing and effects, carried out by the Port Health authorities, and various other matters connected with the annual exodus, occupied the increasing attention of the Muhammadan community and occasionally formed the subject of rather acid criticism. It was asserted that the whole subject of the pilgrimage required more attention than an overworked Police Commissioner could give it, and that more facilities should be accorded to respectable Moslem residents for expressing their views on the details of the traffic and for keeping in touch with the local arrangements for booking and embarkation. Accordingly, the Bombay Government, with a view to disarming criticism and in the hope of giving some relief to the Commissioner, appointed in 1908 a Haj Committee, composed of leading Muhammadan residents of Bombay, with the Commissioner of Police as *ex-officio* President. During the first year of its existence, this Committee did not do very much; but later it developed into a useful consultative body, and gave much assistance to Mr. Gell's successor in matters connected with the comfort of the pilgrims and the local arrangements for housing and disembarkation. On several occasions the members of the Committee subscribed money from their own pockets to relieve cases of distress and secure the repatriation of penniless Moslems stranded in Jeddah.

This period witnessed the preparation of schemes for the housing of the police and the construction of police-stations. In 1902 the City Improvement Trust forwarded to Government for approval plans for stations and residential quarters at Wodehouse road in the Fort and at 1st. Nagpada: and these buildings, together with quarters for the Risaldar of the Mounted Police and stables for the sowars, were completed and occupied in 1906. Meanwhile the Commissioner was pressing for the provision of more accommodation for the constabulary, and he found a powerful ally in the Police Surgeon, Dr. Arthur Powell, who reported in 1905 that the prevalence of pneumonia and consumption in the force was primarily due to the residence of the men in dark, crowded and insanitary *chals*. A little relief was afforded in 1908 by the completion of a block of lines for constables and quarters for native officers in Duncan road, and a set of quarters for European officers, with lines for the men, was also completed at Sussex road in the same year. Much expenditure, however, had still to be incurred before the force could be said to be suitably housed.

Two other important buildings of a different character were provided during Mr. Gell's *régime*—the Northcote Police Hospital and the office of the Protector of Pilgrims. Up to 1866 constables requiring medical treatment were admitted to the Sir J. J. Hospital on Parel road. In that year the stable of the old Hamilton Hotel was assigned as a separate hospital for the police, and was so used till 1870, when the Municipality placed an old workshop in Mazagon at the disposal of the Police Commissioner. This ramshackle building, which accommodated only 35 indoor patients, was totally unsuited for a hospital and was a source of constant and justifiable complaint. Nevertheless the police were forced to put up with it, until Lord Northcote, the Governor, (1900-03) sanctioned the construction of a proper building, accommodating 94 patients, on one of the new roads at Nagpada constructed by the City Improvement Trust. The building was formally opened by Lord Lamington in August, 1904.

The growth of the annual Haj traffic, mentioned in a previous paragraph, rendered accommodation for the office of the Protector of Pilgrims an urgent necessity. A ground-floor building, consisting of a large covered porch and two or three rooms, was therefore built in 1907 in the compound of the Head Police Office and served as the headquarters of the Pilgrim department, until the reorganization of the Criminal Investigation Department by Mr. Edwardes and his Deputy, Mr. F. A. M. H. Vincent, rendered necessary a re-arrangement of the accommodation at headquarters.

Before we describe the disturbances which occurred during Mr. Gell's tenure of office, a word may be said of the courage and resource occasionally shown by Indian constables in the course of their daily duty. In 1903 a havildar was awarded the medal of the Royal Humane Society for rescuing two boys from drowning; a constable received the medal for similar action in the following year; while in 1906 the Society rewarded three constables for saving life in difficult and dangerous circumstances. On several occasions also the Commissioner rewarded constables for actions marked by conspicuous courage or intelligence. These instances serve to support the opinion that under proper leadership the Maratha of the Konkan and the Muhammadan of the Deccan will show plenty of sang-froid in emergencies. Considering that the men received little or no training before being placed on duty in the streets, that they had little or no education, and that they served year after year in a climate which is notoriously enervating and under conditions productive of ill-health, it is greatly to the credit of the police constable that he performed his duty with so few serious mistakes and that he frequently gave proof of personal courage and tenacity. If at times he appeared to cling too closely to the *pan-supari* shops in the vicinity of his post or beat, or to lack alertness in directing traffic, it must be remembered that he was rarely off duty for any length of time, that he had singularly little opportunity for recreation and amusement, and that long hours of point-duty under the Bombay sun would try the strongest constitution.

Twice during Mr. Gell's term of office the peace of the City was broken by rioting at the annual celebration of the Muharram. The first occasion was March 23rd, 1904, the fifth day of the festival, when the ancient antagonism between the Sunni and Shia sects developed into open hostility. The ostensible cause of the disturbance was the determination of the Sunni processionists to play music and beat their tom-toms in front of the Bohra mosque in the notorious Doctor Street. Casual street-fighting between the Bohras and their antagonists occurred daily up to March 27th (the *Katal-Ki-Rat* or night of slaughter), and the aspect of affairs was so ominous that Mr. Gell decided to cancel the license for the *tabut* procession from Rangari *moholla* (i. e. Abdul Rehman street and adjoining lanes), the inhabitants of which had been directly responsible for several assaults upon the Bohras. This order was strongly resented by the general Sunni population, which resolved not to carry out the *tabuts* for immersion on the final day of the festival. As usual, the abandonment of the *tabut* procession released large bodies of hooligans and bad characters, who testified to their annoyance by attacking the police and the general public. At the same time the Bohras were seized by a general panic, the results of which might have been disastrous, and this fact, combined with the open disorder in the streets, led Mr. Gell to summon the military forces to his assistance. The Cheshire Regiment, a Battery of the R. A., the Railway Volunteers, the Bombay Light Horse and H. E. the Governor's Bodyguard were despatched to various points of the disturbed area and picketed the streets until April 1st, when peace was finally restored. The casualties were fortunately few, and serious loss of life was prevented by the speedy arrival of the troops.

Another serious disturbance marred this festival during the last year of Mr. Gell's Commissionership. On the morning of February 13th, 1908, a fracas occurred between a Shia tabut-procession, composed of Julhais, Mughals, Khojas and a few Bohras, and a body of Sunni Muhammadans congregated at a mosque in Falkland road. The police arrested some of the Sunnis who appeared to be the ringleaders in the affray. The news of the encounter spread rapidly to other quarters; and the arrest of their co-sectaries so annoyed the Sunni Muhammadans that they declined to take out their *tabuts* in procession. This resulted, as usual, in letting loose on the streets hundreds of low-class and combative Muhammadans, who usually accompanied the processions, and they straightway proceeded to sow the seeds of disorder in various parts of the bazar. In the hope of averting a catastrophe Mr. Gell gave orders early in the afternoon for the release of the men arrested after the fracas in the morning. But the temper of the mob had by that time been aroused, the cry of *Huriya, Huriya,* was raised, and the ominous stampedes and rushes which usually preceded an outbreak of disorder occurred in the streets and lanes bordering on the Grant and Parel roads. The mob confined itself to these tactics and to spasmodic attacks on the Bohras and other Shias until the late hours of the afternoon, when serious rioting broke out on Parel road. Here the Pathan element joined forces with the mob; shops were looted and set on fire; all traffic was stopped and the tram-cars were stoned. General panic supervened. As the mob was truculent and refused to disperse, Mr. Gell ordered the European police, who were facing the mob in Parel road (Bhendy Bazar), to use their revolvers. The firing put a stop to the actual rioting, but in view of the general demeanour of the crowds, troops were called out in the evening in aid of the civil power and remained on duty in the disturbed quarter until the next day.

These Muharram disturbances, though imposing a severe strain upon the Commissioner and the police force, caused less concern to the general public than the prolonged rioting in the industrial quarter in July, 1908, when more than 400,000 mill-hands broke into open disorder after the conviction of the late Bal Gangadhar Tilak for sedition by the High Court. Tilak had been arrested in Bombay on June 24th on charges arising out of the publication in his paper, the *Kesari,* of articles containing inflammatory comments on the Muzaffarpur outrage, in which Mrs. and Miss Kennedy had been killed by a bomb—the first of a long list of similar outrages in Bengal. The bomb was extolled in these articles as 'a kind of witch-craft, a charm, an amulet', and the *Kesari* delighted in showing that neither 'the supervision of the police' nor 'swarms of detectives' could stop 'these simple playful sports of science.' Whilst professing to deprecate such methods, it threw the responsibility upon Government, which allowed 'keen disappointment to overtake thousands of intelligent persons who have been awakened to the necessity of securing the rights of *Swaraj*'. "Tilak spoke for four whole days in his own defence—21½ hours altogether—but the jury returned a verdict of "Guilty", and he was sentenced to six years' transportation, afterwards commuted on account of his age and health to simple imprisonment at Mandalay."[1]

From the moment of his arrest, Tilak's agents and followers descended upon the mill-area of Bombay and sedulously spread the story that Tilak had been arrested because he was the friend of the industrial workers and had tried to obtain better wages for them. Some of them were reported to have declared during the trial that there would be a day's bloodshed for every year to which he might be sentenced by the Court. Most of the 'jobbers' who control the supply of labour were easily won over, and Tilak's Brahman emissaries from Poona found many co-adjutors among their own caste-men in Bombay, and among the Bhandaris and Konkani Marathas living in Parel, Tardeo, Chinchpugli and Dadar sections. Curiously enough the Ghatis, or Marathas from the Deccan, showed far less interest in the trial of Tilak and far less disposition to violence than their caste-fellows from Ratnagiri and other districts of the western sea-board. The Deccan mill-hands at Sewri, for example, at the very height of the rioting, informed an Englishman with whom they were familiar that he need fear no harm from them, and they confirmed their words by taking no share in the disturbance which lasted for six days. The hostile attitude of the Konkani Marathas was due to the continuous efforts of agitators, and this was particularly the case in the neighbourhood of Currey and De Lisle roads, where special agents from their own districts had been introduced by Tilak's revolutionaries.

The probability of a disturbance was foreseen by the authorities, and Mr. Gell took various precautions to

1. V. Chirol, *Indian Unrest*, pp. 55, 56.

circumscribe the area of the outbreak. British regiments, Indian infantry and cavalry were held in readiness; a barricade was erected on Mayo road leading to the High Court; several officials and non-officials were appointed Special Magistrates and were posted at important points to watch the progress of events, assist the police, and take all feasible measures for securing the peace of the City. The Special Magistrates were a curiously mixed body. Among them were Mr. James Macdonald, a sexagenarian Scotsman, who had served the City for years as a member of the Municipal Corporation; Colonel Cordue, R. E., the Master of the Mint; Mr. Philip Messent, Engineer of the Port Trust; Mr. Arthur Leslie of Messrs. Greaves, Cotton and Co., who filled his pockets with lemon-grass oil for the benefit of the men of the Royal Scots, who were posted at the old police *chauki* in Jacob's Circle and had their bare knees badly bitten by the mosquitoes and other forms of low life which shared the *chauki* with the police-constables; the author of this work, who was at the time enjoying a spell of comparative ease in the literary backwaters of the Bombay City Gazetteer; and last but not least, the Hon. Arthur Hill-Trevor, a commercial free-lance and honorary magistrate, who regarded himself as a sort of Honorary and Supernumerary Deputy Commissioner of Police, and in that capacity executed various blood-curdling manœuvres which caused no little apprehension to his more pacific colleagues.

It so happened that some of the precautions proved superfluous. There was no attempt on the part of the rioters to rush the High Court or even to attend the trial of Tilak: there was no organized attempt to march on the European residential quarter or to attack the European population *en masse*. Although the rioting assumed at times a very threatening character, it was confined wholly to the mill-area, except on one afternoon, when the Bania merchants, employed in the cloth-market of the C division, turned out in force and had to be dispersed by firing. A consideration of all the circumstances of the Tilak riots leads one to infer that the Commissioner was not as well served by his detective agency as he might have been, and that the disturbances might have been more disastrous and have lasted longer, if Tilak's emissaries and agents had had more time at their disposal in which to foster the spirit of violence. By the end of the first day's rioting it was clear that outlying areas like the Fort and Malabar Hill were exposed to no danger, and consequently most of the Special Magistrates gravitated from their original posts to Jacob's Circle, which divided the industrial quarters from the central portion of the City and served as a gathering-ground for the forces of law and order.

Within the mill-district the rioting was fairly continuous and occasionally serious, and isolated Europeans whose duties obliged them to reside in the area north of Jacob's Circle found it wise to vacate their houses for the time being and seek shelter in Mazagon, the Fort and other parts. Much damage was done to mill-property, and in several encounters with the mob the European police were forced to use their revolvers and the troops had to fire in self-defence. The Indian cavalry were stoned from the *chals* on more than one occasion, and small parties of unarmed police fared badly at the hands of the rioters, who had accumulated considerable stores of brick-bats and road-metal at convenient vantage-points.

The Bombay Government, realizing that the trouble was not a sudden and spontaneous outburst of popular feeling and that the rebellious mill-hands were the victims of an unscrupulous agitation, based on malevolent falsehood, had issued strict orders for the avoidance of bloodshed as far as possible: and both the military forces and the police exercised such steady self-restraint that the casualties were relatively few. Nevertheless the continuance of rioting and the dislocation of business in the City set many people wondering whether other methods of restoring peace might not be tried. About the fifth day of the disturbance the Chamber of Commerce sent a deputation to the Governor, to point out the loss sustained by the commercial and trade-interests of the City and to urge upon Government a stronger effort to dissuade the mill-population from violence. The author of this history, who had witnessed the whole sequence of events at Jacob's Circle and had on one occasion accompanied a detachment of the Northampton Regiment to Dadar to protect certain isolated Europeans, had already asked permission of Mr. (afterwards Sir John) Jenkins, Member of Council, to visit the heart of the disturbed area in company with certain Indian gentlemen who had offered their assistance, and endeavour to produce a milder feeling among the mill-hands. The permission was granted. Accordingly the writer, accompanied by the late Rao Bahadur Narayan T. Vaidya, Dr. Dinanath Naik Dandekar and four or five others, visited a large number of mill-hands' *chals* and dwellings in Parel and Dadar, spoke to several groups of mill-hands, and urged them to resume their regular duties. In places the party was met with sullen hostility and with shouts of *Tilak Maharaj ki Jai*, but the eloquence of the Indian members of the party was not without effect, and when Rao Bahadur N.T. Vaidya urged them to substitute *Satya Narayan ki Jai* for their Tilakite war-cry, some of them seemed disposed to accept the suggestion.

Though some were inclined to look askance at their intervention, the efforts of this little peace-party did engender a better feeling, and this, coupled with a natural weariness of prolonged hostilities and the loss of their wages, resulted in the gradual return of tranquillity after the sixth day. By the end of the first week of August, affairs had resumed their normal course, the mill-hands were again at work, and the Bombay Government were at liberty to consider the salient features and lessons of the outbreak. Sir George Clarke, the Governor, was blamed in some quarters for having paid a sympathetic visit, after the close of the riots, to wounded mill-hands in the Sir J. J. Hospital. But his policy in this matter was dictated by an earnest desire to smooth away the bitterness which measures of repression are calculated to provoke, and by a conviction that there had been an absence of contact between the local authorities and the industrial population, which had been permitted to fall completely under the lawless influence of Tilak and his immediate followers. The fact that the disturbances lasted for a whole week invited a doubt whether the police arrangements were as effective as they might have been, and whether indeed a more efficient intelligence organization might not have facilitated a speedier conclusion of the unsatisfactory duties which the military were called upon to perform. An impression prevailed that, although the mill-hands who defied the police and troops had been severely punished, the real authors and fomenters of the disturbances had managed to escape scot-free, and that they could not have enjoyed such immunity, if the police had had their fingers more closely upon the pulse of the City.

So far as concerns the prosecution and conviction of Tilak, Sir George Clarke won "the respect of the vast majority of the community, and although he failed to secure the active support which he might have expected from the 'moderates', there were few of them who did not secretly approve and even welcome his action. Its effects were great and enduring, for Tilak's conviction was a heavy blow to the forces of unrest, at least in the Deccan; and some months later, one of the organs of his party, the *Rashtramat*, reviewing the occurrences of the year, was fain to admit that 'the sudden removal of Mr. Tilak's towering personality threw the whole province into dismay and unnerved the other leaders".[1]

Having thus secured the discomfiture of the revolutionary party in Western India, the Governor applied himself to the problem of the Bombay City Police administration, which appeared to him to need revision,

1. V. Chirol, *Indian Unrest*, p. 57.

not only in response to the general findings of the Police Commission, but also by reason of its apparent failure to keep closely in touch with political intrigue, such as that which precipitated the riots of July 1908. Apart from the mere question of numbers and pay, the force appeared to the Governor to be working on somewhat obsolete lines and to need keying up to the pitch at which it might cope more successfully both with its regular duties of watch and ward and with the large amount of confidential investigation necessitated by the rapid and alarming growth of political unrest and sedition. These were the main reasons underlying the appointment of the Morison Committee, which has been described in an earlier paragraph. One of the most important sections of that committee's report was concerned with the reorganization of the old detective branch of the police-force, hereafter to be called the Criminal Investigation Department (C. I. D.), upon which devolved the task of watching the trend of political movements and of accumulating knowledge of the antecedents and actions of the chief fomenters of unrest.

The work of a police-officer in an Indian city has always been extremely arduous, and few men in these days are able to bear the strain for many years without some loss of vitality and health. There is little doubt that the extra work and anxiety entailed by the Royal Visit of 1905, which was followed a few days later by the arrival of Lord Minto and the departure of Lord Curzon, had much to do with the temporary breakdown of health which obliged Mr. Gell to take furlough in 1906; while the strain inevitably imposed upon him by the Muharram and Tilak riots of 1908 was partly the cause of his again taking leave to England in the early part of 1909. In doing so, his long service in the City came to an end: for by the time his leave had expired, his successor was in the midst of a comprehensive reorganization scheme, which would have suffered in the event of his reversion to his own grade in the Indian Civil Service.

In order, therefore, to enable him to complete his full period of pensionable service, Mr. Gell, on his return from England, was appointed Deputy Inspector-General of Police for the Presidency and a little later for Sind. It was in Sind that he completed his official career, and from Karachi that he sailed finally for England. His long connexion with the City of Bombay is commemorated, though not perhaps adequately, in the name of one of the newer streets opened by the City Improvement Trust in the neighbourhood of Ripon road. Memories of his equability of temper and his impartiality are still cherished by the older officers and men of the police-force, who pay a willing tribute to his character as an officer and a gentleman.

CHAPTER IX

Mr. S. M. Edwardes, C.S.I., C.V.O.

1909—1916

Mr. S. M. Edwardes, who succeeded Mr. Gell as head of the Bombay City Police Force, was the first member of the Indian Civil Service to hold that appointment. He had previously held various appointments in Bombay ranging from Assistant to the Collector and Chief Inspector of Factories to acting Municipal Commissioner, and had acquired considerable knowledge of the population and past history of Bombay by his work as Census Officer in 1901 and later as Compiler of the Gazetteer. Shortly after the Tilak riots in 1908, he was nominated a member of the Morison Committee which, as previously stated, was appointed by the Bombay Government to consider the working of the urban police administration and make proposals for its future organization.

This Committee, which met in the Secretariat, directed particular attention to the provision of properly equipped police stations, to the reconstitution and enlargement of the detective branch, hereafter to be known as the C. I. D., to the creation of a trained Indian staff for the investigation of crime in the Divisions, and to the numbers and personnel of the European and Indian branches of the force. The Committee came to the conclusion from the facts and evidence before them that in dealing with political crime and seditious movements, planned, promoted and carried out by an Indian *intelligentsia*, the police were handicapped by the absence of educated Indians in the subordinate ranks of the force, and that the investigation of ordinary crime by the divisional police suffered from being in the hands of an old-fashioned agency, which conducted its inquiries in a multiplicity of small and sometimes obscure *chaukis* and kept no proper record of its cases. Concentration of the staff in a definite number of properly-equipped stations in each division, and the inclusion in the force of a new cadre of Indian officers for the divisional investigation of crime were two obvious desiderata, upon which the Committee laid particular stress. They decided also that the time had arrived to place the C. I. D. under the immediate control of a gazetted officer of the Imperial Police, who would occupy the position of a Deputy Commissioner, leaving the existing Deputy Commissioner to deal with the divisional police and with the large amount of miscellaneous work requiring the attention of the head-quarters staff. Proposals, of a more or less tentative character, were also made regarding the numbers, grading and duties of the European police, the recruitment of Indian constables, and the numbers and work of the Harbour, Docks and Mounted Police.

After drafting the report of the Committee and arranging for its submission to Government in October, 1908, Mr. Edwardes took leave to England. While there, he received an intimation from the Bombay Government of their intention to appoint him Commissioner of Police *vice* Mr. Gell, who proposed to take leave in 1909. He was at the same time instructed to visit Scotland Yard and study at first hand the organization of the Metropolitan Police. Armed with a letter from the Home Office to the Chief Commissioner, Sir Edward Henry, Mr. Edwardes accordingly spent some time in the early part of 1909 in acquainting himself with the distribution of work and the machinery for the prevention and detection of crime in a typical London police division, with the details of the Metropolitan beat-system, with the work of the constables' training-school in Westminster, with the organization of the Finger Print Bureau, and with the staffing, equipment, structural features and general management of one of the latest and most up-to-date London police-stations. The knowledge thus acquired was of the greatest value, when his own proposals for the reorganization of the Bombay City Police were under-preparation.

Mr. Edwardes assumed charge of the Commissioner's office on May 7th, 1909, with Mr. R. M. Phillips as his Deputy Commissioner and Superintendent Sloane as head of the Criminal Investigation Department. The former was succeeded in July by Mr. Hayter, who made way in September for Mr. Gadney. The latter served as Deputy Commissioner until November, 1913, when his place was taken by Mr. O. Allen Harker, who held the appointment until after the expiry of Mr. Edwardes' term of office. In pursuance of the recommendations of the Morison Committee, an additional appointment of Deputy Commissioner in charge of the C. I. D. was sanctioned by G. R. J. D. 3253 of June 8th, 1909; and, Superintendent Sloane having been promoted to the cadre of the Imperial Police and transferred to a district, the new post was given to Mr. F. A. M. H. Vincent, son of the former Commissioner of Police, who held it until the beginning of 1913, when he was appointed Deputy Director of Criminal Intelligence at Simla. He was succeeded in Bombay by Mr. F. C. Griffith, who remained in charge of the C. I. D. during the remainder of Mr. Edwardes' term of office. Both Mr. Vincent and Mr. Griffith subsequently succeeded in turn to the Commissioner's appointment. In 1914 a third appointment of Deputy Commissioner was sanctioned by G. R. J. D. 9249 of December 19th, 1914, under the style and title of Deputy Commissioner of Police for the Port of Bombay. Mr. G. S. Wilson was chosen for this post and became responsible, under the general authority of the Commissioner, for all work connected with the Harbour and Dock Police and the Pilgrim Traffic. This period thus witnessed the permanent appointment of three Deputy Commissioners in place of a single officer of that rank, and the consequent delegation to them by the Commissioner of much of the work which he had hitherto been expected to perform without adequate assistance.

Mr. Edwardes' appointment was not received favourably at first by the members of the Imperial Police Service, who naturally felt some resentment at such a post being given to one who was not a professional police-officer. This feeling led to the submission of memorials on the subject to the Bombay Government, who were able without difficulty to justify their departure from the usual practice. The discontent also communicated itself to the rank and file of the City police, who during the first few months of Mr. Edwardes' *régime* displayed a spirit of captious criticism, which was fanned at last by a few malcontents into overt disobedience. The movement culminated on January 7th, 1910, in the refusal of a certain number of Indian constables to receive their pay. The Commissioner, who had kept himself informed of the course of the movement, had arranged with the European officers of the Divisions what action should be taken in the event of open insubordination. The men who declined to accept their pay were therefore marched immediately to the Head Police Office and, after inquiry into their conduct, were dismissed from the force. This action completely quashed the movement, which was based upon no real grievance and was designed merely to cause trouble to a Commissioner, whose policy and plans they had been taught to regard with suspicion.

The strength and cost of the City Police Force underwent much alteration during this period of seven years, in consequence of the reorganization scheme prepared by the Commissioner. His proposals for the future constitution and character of the force, which were submitted in July, 1910, were sanctioned by the Government of India in September, 1911; but owing to very heavy work connected with the visit of Their Majesties the King and Queen in November of that year, the scheme was not actually introduced until the beginning of 1912.

As early as 1909, however, certain changes were made in consonance with the proposals of the Morison Committee, and to meet emergent requirements, which resulted in an increase of the total number to 2,408. This total included additions to the Dockyard police, temporary sanitary police for service under the Port Health Officer, temporary constables for traffic-duty at various railway level crossings, and finally the revised strength of the C. I. D., which was fixed by G. R. J. D. 2708 of May 10th, 1909, at 1 Superintendent, 6 Inspectors, 7 Sub-Inspectors, 23 Head Constables and 41 Constables. In 1910 an additional Inspector was sanctioned for the Motor Vehicles department; and 9 Indian sub-inspectors, 3 head constables and 9 constables were added to the force, to enable the Commissioner to introduce tentatively in three areas the new divisional organization which formed the salient feature of his administrative proposals. Thus by 1911 the force numbered 2,505, which was equivalent to a proportion of one policeman to every 394 of population, and cost annually, inclusive of temporary police and contingent charges, Rs. 10,93,351. In 1913, when the reorganization was well in hand, the total strength of the force stood at 2,844 and cost Rs. 12,73,834; while at the end of 1915, a few months before Mr. Edwardes relinquished office, the total number, inclusive of a small temporary staff for watching trans-frontier Pathans in the City, was 3,011, and the annual cost amounted to Rs. 13,37,208. The proportion of police to population at this date was 1 to 327, which compared unfavourably with the proportions in Calcutta and London. Had the Commissioner's first proposals been sanctioned without alteration, the proportion of police to population in Bombay would have been far more favourable; for he had worked out a complete beat-system on the London model for the whole of the City. The number of men, however, required for this purpose was naturally large, and as the Bombay Government were compelled by the Government of India to restrict the additional annual cost of the force to 2½ lakhs of rupees, the Commissioner was obliged to jettison the beat-system and utilize the available funds in other directions, such as perfecting the divisional machinery for the investigation of crime, increasing the number of fixed traffic posts, and augmenting the inadequate pay of the European police.

This force of just over 3,000 men was distributed among the following divisions at the close of 1916:—

Division	Sub-divisions or Sections
A	Colaba, Fort South, Fort North, Esplanade
B	Mandvi, Chakla, Umarkhadi, Dongri
C	Market and Dhobi Talao, Bhuleshwar and Khara Talao
D	Khetwadi, Girgaum, Chaupati, Walkeshwar
E	Mazagaon, Tarwadi, Kamathipura, New Nagpada, Mahalakshmi, Jacob's Circle
F	Parel, Dadar, Matunga, Sion
G	Mahim, Worli
H and I	Harbour and Docks
L	Head Quarters Armed and Unarmed Police
M	Mounted Police
N	The Government Dockyard

and The Criminal Investigation Department (formerly the K division),

With the appointment of Mr. F. A. M. H. Vincent as Deputy Commissioner, C. I. D., and the increase in its personnel, the Criminal Investigation Department entered upon a period of remarkable activity. The staff was divided into four branches—Political, Foreign, Crime, and Miscellaneous—each in control of one or more Inspectors; work-books were introduced, which fixed responsibility upon individual officers for cases entrusted to them for inquiry and served as a check upon delay in the submission of final reports of investigations; a confidential strong-room was provided, and the card index system and upright filing of records were substituted for the old methods in vogue at this date in most official departments. In addition to the investigation of cases, some of the more remarkable of which will be mentioned hereafter, the department made confidential inquiries, often of a delicate character, into political, religious and social movements; it scrutinized plays for performance licenses, amending or rejecting those that were objectionable; it took vigorous action under the Press Act, confiscating on occasions as many as twenty-one thousand copies of proscribed books; it maintained a constant watch upon the arrivals and departures of steamers, assisted the Excise authorities, collaborated with the police of other districts and provinces, supervised and, if necessary, prohibited the songs sung by the *melas* at the annual Ganpati celebration, and performed an immense amount of confidential work in connexion with the Muharram. It also assisted or secured the repatriation of all manner of destitute persons stranded in Bombay, including English theatrical artistes, Arabs belonging to French territories, ladies from Mauritius, Bengali seamen, Pathan labourers expelled from Ceylon, and deportees from the Transvaal.

The establishment at the beginning of 1911 of a "Police Gazette", appearing thrice in the twenty-four hours and containing full details of all reported crimes, persons wanted, property stolen or lost, etc., was a further step in the direction of increased efficiency. Prior to this date, when a case of theft occurred, the first duty of the Inspector, in whose jurisdiction it took place, was to prepare with his own hand thirty or forty notices for dispatch to other police-stations in the City. Much valuable time was thus wasted; and when the notices were ready, several constables had to be released from their proper duties to act as messengers. Under the system introduced in 1911 the duty of the sectional officer consisted simply in telephoning full details to the Deputy Commissioner C. I. D., who arranged for their insertion in the next issue of the "Gazette", copies of which were delivered at every police station within a few hours of the occurrence. The arrangements were adapted from the system followed in London and effected a great saving of time and trouble in the divisions. In 1915 the Police Notice Office, composed of a European Inspector and an Indian head constable, circulated in this way nearly 10,000 paragraphs and 67 supplements dealing with murders, thefts, deserters and persons wanted, and also published and circulated to the divisions forty pages of special orders concerned with daily routine.

Another salient feature of the reorganization, as mentioned above, was the creation of a special agency for the divisional investigation of crime. This was dependent upon the provision of properly-equipped police stations of a definite type, recommended by Mr. Edwardes, comprising the necessary offices, charge-room, cells, quarters for the European and Indian staff, and barracks for the constabulary. The scheme, as sanctioned, contemplated the provision of 17 stations of this character. At the date when Mr. Edwardes was appointed Commissioner, none of the existing police-stations fulfilled these requirements, and in some divisions paucity of accommodation directly hampered the daily work of the police. In 1911, for example, the station of the Khetwadi section of the D division was described as practically non-existent. The lease of a building having expired, and no alternative accommodation being available, the Inspector was holding his office in the dressing-room of an Indian theatre in Grant road, the station-stores and constables' kit-boxes were temporarily placed in a tea-shop in Falkland road, and the two European officers of the section were forced to reside in very poor quarters in an adjoining section. Most of the older stations were very inconvenient and insanitary. The only office consisted of one of the sectional Inspector's dwelling-rooms or of a portion of a verandah screened off; prisoners and witnesses were herded together on the stairs or in the street; the residence was surrounded by old-fashioned and odoriferous latrines; and every odd corner was choked with kit-boxes and with the recumbent forms of constables taking a rest before going on duty.

By the end of 1910, however, a complete programme for new stations had been prepared, and sanctioned by Government, and a commencement had been made in Colaba, Nagpada and Agripada, where the newer police-stations erected by the Improvement Trust were subjected to structural alterations and additions, in order to make them conform with the plan adapted from the London model. Each of these stations was equipped with a staff composed of one Inspector, one Deputy Inspector, three Indian Sub-Inspectors for criminal investigation, plain-clothes constables and a clerical staff; the first information sheet, case-diary and other records used by the District Police were so adapted to urban requirements as to secure a complete record of every case taken up by the police; and the time-table of duties was arranged so that at any moment during the twenty-four hours an English-knowing officer, with power to record complaints and commence inquiries, would be found in the general charge-room of the station. At the outset most of the Indian Sub-Inspectors were chosen from among the few English-knowing Jemadars and Havildars, already in the force; but from 1910 onwards a regular supply of such officers was secured by choosing young Indians of good middle-class standing and deputing them to the Provincial Police Training School at Nasik for an eighteen months' course of tuition in law and police-work.

At the beginning of 1913 the Commissioner opened two more stations on the new model at Princess Street—a building erected by the Improvement Trust in 1910, and at Maharbaudi: and two more in 1914 in the new buildings of the Harbour and Dock police at Mody Bay and

Frere road respectively, which were completed and occupied in January. At the beginning of January, 1916, three more stations were established under the reorganization scheme at Khetwadi, Hughes road, and the Esplanade, while at the close of the same year similar stations were organized in the new buildings erected at Gamdevi, Lamington road and Palton road. Thus, by the end of 1916 thirteen out of the seventeen model police-stations, originally proposed by the Commissioner, had been opened with a full complement of officers and men, while plans had been approved for similar accommodation in Mahim, Parel and other places in the northern portion of the Island of Bombay. Where it was found impossible to build full residential accommodation for both officers and men on the site allotted for these new stations, ancillary accommodation schemes were prepared, which, when completed, would ensure the proper housing of the majority of the force as it existed at the date of Mr. Edwardes' departure.

A sustained effort was made during these years to teach English to the Indian constabulary, with the object of giving the men themselves a better chance of promotion and enabling them to hold their own more confidently with the large English-speaking population. In 1910 the number of officers, exclusive of Europeans, able to read and write was 127, of whom only 36 were literate in English, while literate constables, of whom only one or two knew English, numbered 584. In July 1911 the Commissioner commenced sending a chosen number of Muhammadan and Hindu constables to two free night-schools for instruction in English and one vernacular language. The success attending this experiment led the Bombay Government to sanction a proposal to open an English school for constables at the Head Police Office, under a qualified teacher from one of the official training-schools maintained by the Educational Department. This school was attended by 150 constables from the various branches of the force, who were given a three years' course of tuition in English, and on Saturdays attended lectures on their duty to the public, their powers under the Police Act, and matters of simple hygiene. In 1913 the number of men attending the school had risen to 200, and the master had been forced to obtain gratuitous assistance in teaching the various classes. The question of accommodation also became urgent, and during 1915 and 1916 the classes had to be assembled in the Elphinstone Middle School, which the educational authorities allowed the police to use during the early morning and evening hours. The men, who were encouraged to study by the grant of small rewards and occasionally of promotion, if they were successful in the periodical examinations, derived distinct advantage from the school-course, and the number of constables literate in the English language showed a steady increase between 1911 and 1916. In the latter year 846 constables were reported to be able to read and write, and 72 of them were literate in English. Connected with the subject of education was the foundation of a fund in the name of the Commissioner—the S. M. E. Memorial Fund—subscribed by Hindu and Muhammadan residents, with the object of assisting Indian constables of the force to educate their sons. The proposal was made in the first instance by Mr. Kazi Kabiruddin, a barrister and Justice of the Peace, and at his instance sufficient funds were subsequently provided to admit of the grant of monthly scholarships and stipends to the sons of constables attending primary schools maintained by the Municipal Corporation.

A large amount of routine work devolved upon the police under the Arms, Explosives, Petroleum and Poisons Acts. Under the Arms Act licenses of various kinds were granted or cancelled, the shops and store-rooms of licensed dealers were regularly inspected and their stocks checked, and constant inquiries, numbering several thousand annually, were made to verify purchases from local dealers and trace the whereabouts of fire-arms. In 1911, just before the arrival of Their Majesties the King and Queen, five revolvers were stolen from a licensed dealer's shop. The C. I. D. were successful in recovering the arms and in obtaining the conviction of the thieves: but in consideration of the approach of the Royal Visit, the Commissioner decided to take charge of the entire stock of arms and ammunition held by five Indian dealers, and kept it in deposit in the Head Police Office until after the departure of Their Majesties. Under the Explosives Act licenses were issued for manufacture, possession and sale; and magazines for the storage of explosives were regularly inspected by the special branch maintained for this purpose at head-quarters. Similar duties were carried out under the Petroleum Act; while from April 1st, 1909, the Police became responsible for licensing the sale of poisons and checking stocks,—duties which up to that date had been performed by the Municipality. The task of licensing theatres and granting performance licenses, which was transferred to the Arms department at the close of 1909, imposed a heavy additional burden on the special staff. Most of the theatres at this date were devoid of proper exits and of means of protection against fire, and these seven years witnessed a continuous struggle to secure the erection of fire-proof staircases etc. and the provision of fire-proof drop-curtains. Fortunately the Police were able to obtain the help of the Chief of the Fire-brigade and of the Government engineering and electrical experts, in deciding what improvements were essential in each case, and it was chiefly due to this collaboration that a better fire-service had been installed by 1913 in each of the thirteen theatres of the City, and that many important structural alterations in both theatres and cinematographs had been introduced by the close of 1916. Perhaps the most notable achievement of the headquarters staff under Chief Inspector M. J. Giles was the preparation of a set of theatre rules, applicable to all structures used for public performances, which were brought into force in August 1914, and gave the police power to insist upon the provision of fire-appliances, water-supply, exits, and fire-proof materials. As mentioned in a previous paragraph, the C. I. D. was made responsible for the scrutiny of plays, for which a performance license was required, and licenses were granted only to such plays as were declared by that department to be unobjectionable on political, moral or general grounds.

The growth in the number of motor-vehicles continued unchecked and ultimately necessitated the promulgation of new rules under the Motor Vehicles Act in 1915. In 1909, the total number of motor-vehicles registered since 1905 was 1,295, while in 1915 this figure had increased to 4,947. But a good many of these gradually disappeared in the course of ten years, and the actual number estimated to be on the roads in 1915 was 2,482 as compared with only 814 in 1909. Heavy motor-vehicles of the lorry type also appeared during this period and numbered 70 in 1915. This increase of motor-traffic synchronized with, and was partly responsible for, a steady increase in the number of street accidents. While reckless driving was unquestionably the cause of many accidents, despite energetic action in several directions to prevent it, the large majority of the casualties reported from year to year were the outcome of that carelessness and lack of alertness on the part of the average Indian pedestrian, with which all who have driven cars or carriages in Bombay are only too well acquainted. Accustomed as they are to the peace of a sequestered country life, many of the foot-passengers in the streets of the city seem totally unable to exercise any caution or to acquire the habit of keeping to the side of the road, while in the case of the mill-workers, whom one meets in Parel and elsewhere, the sense of hearing seems to have been permanently dulled by the constant rattle and clatter of the machinery at which they labour during the greater part of the day.

The Haj traffic continued to expand between 1909 and 1911, the total number of pilgrims who left Bombay for Jeddah in those years being 19,748 and 21,965 respectively. From 1912 the numbers commenced to decline until the year after the outbreak of the War, when the traffic virtually ceased altogether. The period witnessed a struggle on the part of a British shipping-firm to secure the monoply of the Red Sea trade, including the pilgrim traffic, by ousting the few Muhammadan-owned vessels which had hitherto catered for the pilgrims. The firm in question was unquestionably in a position to offer better vessels and a better organization for the return journey than the Indian ship-owners: but one or two of the latter resented the effort to drive them out of the traffic, with the result that the Commissioner of Police and the Pilgrim department, who endeavoured to act in a strictly neutral manner, ran the risk of blame from both parties for showing undue preference to their rivals. At the moment of the Declaration of War all the vessels engaged in the traffic were owned by the British firm, except one or at most two which belonged to a well-known Muhammadan resident. It might have been supposed that, considering the wholly Islamic character of the pilgrimage, a British firm would have acquiesced in the continued presence of a Muhammadan-owned vessel, and have trusted to time and the ordinary economic law for its ultimate disappearance from the Jeddah route. Such, however, was not the case; and at the instance of the local manager of the firm, a pushing Scot from Aberdeen, the Bombay Government was asked practically to insist upon the Commissioner and the Pilgrim department refusing all facilities to the Muhammadan ship-owner to sell his tickets and dispatch his vessel. The outbreak of War in 1914, and the consequent cessation of the traffic to and from Jeddah, solved a dispute which for some time imposed additional work upon the Police and Pilgrim authorities.

The Finger Print Bureau steadily maintained its

efficiency and had compiled a record of more than 45,000 slips by the end of 1915. At the request of the municipal authorities, it commenced about 1912 to take the finger-impressions of hundreds of candidates for employment as sweepers in the Health department, and was able to prove annually from its records that a certain proportion of these people had previous convictions under the Penal Code. In another direction—revolver-practice by the European police—a considerable improvement was effected. Up to 1914 it was customary to arrange for the practice in a field at the back of the China Mill at Sewri, which was sufficiently remote and secluded to obviate danger to the public. But the distance of the site from the centre of the City rendered the regular attendance of all officers practically impossible, and in consequence, on the rare occasions when the European police were called upon to use their revolvers at disturbances, their shooting was inclined to be a trifle erratic. In the Muharram riots of 1908, for example, when Mr. Gell ordered the European officers to fire on the mob in Bhendy Bazar, a Parsi who was watching the rioting from the window of a third upper-storey was unfortunately killed by a revolver-shot, directed at the crowd in the street. To ensure more regular practice by all officers, therefore, the Commissioner obtained the approval of Government to the erection of a safety revolver range in the compound of the Head Police Office, which was opened in September, 1914.

Before dealing with the record of crime, a brief reference is desirable to the extraordinary volume of miscellaneous work performed under the orders of the Commissioner. Derelict children were constantly being picked up in the streets by the divisional police and forwarded to the Head Office, when the Commissioner had to make the best arrangements he could for their maintenance and welfare; penniless women and children were repatriated to various parts of India, to Persia, Mauritius, Egypt, South Africa and Singapore, with funds collected by the Police Office for each individual case from charitable townspeople; penurious women were assisted to get their daughters married, and on one occasion a Muhammadan and his wife, who desired a divorce and applied for police assistance, were granted facilities for the ceremony at police headquarters. On another occasion the Commissioner was asked to assist in the rebuilding of a mosque belonging to the Sidis or African Musalmans of Tandel Street, and was able to obtain the necessary funds from several well-to-do Muhammadans in the city. The Police dealt also with a large number of lunatics; they traced deserters from the Army and Navy; they made inquiries into the condition of second-class hotels and drinking-bars in the European quarter and took action, when necessary, in consultation with the Excise authorities; they dealt with a very large number of prostitutes under the Police Act. The number of summonses which they were called upon to serve annually on behalf of magisterial courts in Bombay and other Provinces was enormous, and their work in connexion with the grant of certificates of identity to persons proceeding to Europe, with the grant of passes for processions and for playing music in the streets, and of permits to enter the Ballard Pier on the arrival and departure of the English mail-steamer, was heavy and continuous. Appeals for unofficial assistance from private individuals and from societies like the League of Mercy, engaged in rescue-work among women, were also never refused. Miscellaneous activities of this varied type formed no small portion of the annual task of the force and were rendered effective by the close collaboration of the staff at headquarters, the C. I. D., and the divisional police.

The difficulty of providing suitable shelter and guardianship for the many derelict girls of tender age found wandering in the streets by the police led directly to the foundation by the Commissioner of the Abdulla Haji Daud Bavla Muhammadan Girls' Orphanage. With the possible exception of one or two Christian missionary institutions, to which it would have been impolitic on political and religious grounds to send children, no organization or society existed in 1909, which was prepared to take charge of homeless girls. Consequently, many little waifs gravitated into the brothels of the city or were gradually absorbed in the floating criminal population. Moreover, when a child was found in the streets, homeless and friendless, the police had no shelter to offer her except the cells at the sectional police-station; and these, being regularly filled with the dregs of the criminal population, were a most undesirable environment for girls of tender years. As caste-prejudices offered peculiar obstacles to any scheme for the benefit of Hindu girls belonging to the Shudra class, the Commissioner determined to concentrate his attention upon a home for Muhammadan girls, and accordingly drew up a scheme and issued an appeal, which was widely circulated among the Muhammadan community. The appeal was favourably received, and about 2 lakhs of rupees were collected within a few weeks. To this sum were added more than 3 lakhs from the estate of the late Abdulla Haji Daud Bavla, whose executors offered the amount on condition that the orphanage should bear his name, that his trustees should be represented on the managing committee of the orphanage, and that the objects, constitution and maintenance etc. of the orphanage should be embodied in a legal deed of trust. At the request of the Commissioner, the Bombay Government agreed to become a party to the deed and bound themselves to appoint the Commissioner of Police, or any other of their officers resident for the time being in Bombay, as chairman of the board of trustees of the orphanage. The legal preliminaries having been completed and the funds duly invested in gilt-edged securities, a suitable building was taken on a lease, and furnished at the expense of a philanthropic Muhammadan merchant, and in December, 1910, the orphanage was formally opened by Sir George Clarke (now Lord Sydenham) and Lady Clarke. The institution soon justified its existence; the number of girl-inmates steadily increased, their physical health and welfare being under the general supervision of a trustworthy Englishwoman, and their religious exercises and elementary lessons being given by a Mullani and her assistants. The problem of the girls' future was solved in the only feasible way by arranging for their marriage with Muhammadans of their own class, as soon as they reached the age of maturity. These hymeneal arrangements were made by a chosen officer of the C. I. D., Khan Saheb M. F. Taki, in consultation with the *jamats* and leaders of the various Musalman sections. Experience has proved that the establishment of institutions like this Muhammadan Girls' Orphanage is an essential preliminary to any serious effort to combat the deplorable traffic in children, which still flourishes in India and constitutes the chief means of recruitment for the brothels of the larger towns and cities.

This period witnessed a steady increase in crime up to 1915, when the stringent measures taken during the pendency of the War to clear the City of undesirables imposed a notable check upon the normal increase in reported crime. Previous to that date the rapid increase in recorded crime was the natural result of the changes which took place in the force after 1909, and particularly of the improvement in registration which followed the introduction of the new divisional police-stations. Not only did these stations offer increased facilities for the reporting and detection of crime, but it was also impossible under the new system for cases to escape registration and final inclusion in the returns. The improvement in the registration of cases was manifested also in a marked diminution of the number of complaints classed as made under a misapprehension of law or fact. By 1916 the sanctioned strength of the police force had been augmented by one-third since 1906, and this fact by itself would have sufficed to account for a large increase in the amount of crime brought to light. When coupled with the reorganization of the various police-stations, each of which was furnished with a strong registering and investigating staff, the increase in recorded crime became inevitable. It was likewise due to more accurate estimates of the value of property stolen that the percentage of recovery declined from 56 in 1908 to about 40 in succeeding years.

Murder and attempts at murder were still deplorably frequent, including cases of infanticide which are extremely difficult to detect in an Oriental city. The number of murder cases varied from 16 in 1909 to 31 in 1910, 25 in 1911, 31 in 1912, and 24 in both 1913 and 1915. The largest number, 35, occurred in 1914. The most notable murder was that of a young and wealthy Bhattia widow, residing in her own house on Malabar Hill. Her husband, Lakhmidas Khimji, who had died some time previously in circumstances which gave rise to ill-founded rumour, had been a well-known figure in Indian commercial circles. His widow Jamnabai, was brutally strangled by a gang of six men from northern India, two of whom belonged to well-known criminal tribes in the United Provinces and a third was a night-watchman in the employ of a Jain resident on Malabar Hill. At first there appeared to be no clue whatever to the crime; but a few days after its occurrence the Commissioner received an anonymous letter in Hindi, which was translated for him by the Subehdar of the Armed Police, who happened to be a north-Indian Brahman conversant with that language. The letter, which was written by one of the criminals in revenge for not receiving what he regarded as a fair share of the ornaments stolen from the widow's house, gave sufficient details to enable the Police to arrest five of the gang the same evening. The sixth accused was subsequently arrested at Bassein. All of them were placed on trial for murder and convicted.

By the year 1909, the vice of cocaine-eating had

attained an extraordinary hold upon the lower classes of the population. Women and even children had fallen victims to a habit which plainly exercised a deplorable effect upon their health and morals. The supplies of the drug came in the first instance from Germany in packets bearing the name of Merk, and were frequently smuggled into India in ways that defied detection. Moreover the traffic in the drug, which was international in character, was so cleverly organized that it was practically impossible to trace and prosecute the importers and distributors. Action was therefore confined to prosecuting the smaller fry for the offences of illicit sale and possession, and the majority of such cases occurred in the notorious Nal Bazar area of the C division, which for the last thirty or forty years has sheltered a large population of disreputables. The Police were not held primarily responsible for the control of the cocaine-traffic. This duty devolved upon the Collector of Bombay, who maintained a large and well-paid excise staff for the purpose.[1] But the obligation which rested on the police to assist the excise authorities as far as possible, and the direct stimulus to crime provided by the cocaine-habit, rendered the question of combating the traffic of more than ordinary importance. With this in view, the Commissioner in 1909 put a special police-cordon on the area devoted to the traffic for about six weeks. This produced satisfactory results for the time being, but had to be abandoned, to allow of the men reverting to their regular duties which suffered by their absence. In 1911 a second attempt was made to restrict the evil by placing a European Inspector and a staff of constables on special duty in the C division for a period of about two months, during which nearly 600 individuals

1. Prior to 1913 the Excise authorities were not empowered to prosecute offenders in the Courts. The Police had to conduct all prosecutions. From the year mentioned the Excise department was given the necessary powers.

were caught and convicted by the courts. These incursions into the area of the retail-traffic were not the only successes achieved by the police. In 1911 the Dock Police arrested an Austrian steward of the S. S. *Africa* with 300 grains of cocaine concealed in the soles of his boots; in 1912 the Superintendent of the Harbour Police secured the arrest of a fireman from a German merchant-ship with 40 lbs. of the drug, valued at Rs. 45,500, in his possession; another large consignment, valued at Rs. 17,000 was traced by Khan Saheb M. H. Taki and Khan Saheb F. M. Taki of the C. I. D. to a house in Doctor Street in 1913; and on two occasions Indian constables on duty in the Docks arrested on suspicion persons belonging to vessels in the harbour, with large quantities of the drug concealed on their person. It cannot be asserted, however, that these arrests and prosecutions secured any real diminution of the traffic from abroad. They did upset the local market for the drug, and interfered temporarily with the supply of the tiny paper packets sold in the darker corners of the C division. The traffickers were not thereby daunted, for when the real article was difficult to procure, they palmed off powdered magnesia and Epsom salts on their unfortunate victims, who were naturally unable to complain of the deception. The first real check to the traffic was provided by the drastic restrictions on imports and exports imposed after the declaration of War in 1914, and by the sudden cessation of the continental steamship companies' traffic between Europe and the East. At a comparatively recent date the question of the traffic in cocaine has been discussed at Geneva under the auspices of the League of Nations, and the view seems to be generally accepted that the evil can only be adequately countered by stringent supervision of the primary sources of supply and joint action on the part of all the States concerned.

Of the many important criminal cases successfully investigated by the Police during these seven years, a few deserve special mention. In 1910 and 1911 some very seditious books were brought to the notice of the Bombay Government by certain persons to whom they had been sent anonymously. In the course of their inquiries the Police discovered a large store of these books at Navsari in the Baroda State, and also secured proof that the books were printed at Mehsana in the same territory. A prominent Indian pleader of Kaira, who was concerned in their distribution, was prosecuted and duly convicted. H. H. the Gaekwar of Baroda was in England at the time of the inquiry; but on his return he deported the author of the books, who was one of his own subjects, for a period of five years. In 1912 the police successfully dealt with a swindler named Amratlal, who had victimised a firm of jewellers in Germany to the extent of nearly 2 lakhs of rupees, and they also detected the perpetrator of a series of thefts on board the P. and O. Company's ships, including a case of tampering with the mails. In the following year the premises of the well-known firm of Messrs Ewart, Latham and Company were destroyed by fire. Immediately after the fire, a stolen cheque filled in for Rs. 10,826 and bearing a forged signature, was presented at a bank for payment and cashed. One of the firm's employés was eventually arrested and charged with the offences of theft, cheating and forgery, the police investigation establishing also the moral certainty that the accused had set fire to the office in the hope of obliterating all trace of his crime. The accused was committed to the Sessions, where a peculiarly stupid jury, failing to appreciate the evidence, brought in a verdict of "not guilty." The presiding Judge discharged the accused and passed severe comments on the perversity displayed by the jury. A case, which contained elements of both tragedy and comedy, concerned the marriage of a Koli girl, about 9 years old, to a sexagenarian Bania. Three Hindus, acting on the principle that love is blind, falsely represented that the girl was a Bania, and thereby induced the elderly Lothario to pay Rs. 1,500 for the privilege of wedding the girl. After the marriage the old gentleman discovered the deception practised upon him, and made a formal complaint to the police, who traced the three culprits and secured the conviction of two of them.

In 1914 the embezzlement of Rs. 1,000, representing the fees paid by students at the Government Law School, led to the arrest and conviction of a clerk on the school staff, who was proved in the course of the police-inquiry to have embezzled no less than Rs. 12,000 between the years 1902 and 1912. At the request of the police of the United Provinces, two charges of filing false civil suits, with the object of avoiding payment of sums due by them, were successfully proved against natives of upper India; and these were followed by an equally long and intricate inquiry into a case of cheating, in which three Hindus, one of whom had a local reputation as a palmist and astrologer, persuaded two Bhandaris of Bombay to pay them Rs. 4,000, on condition that they would use their supposed influence with the excise authorities to obtain two liquor-licenses for their dupes. In 1915 the Bohra thief and house-breaker, Tyebali, whose conviction during Mr. Gell's *régime* has already been mentioned, completed his term of imprisonment and recommenced his thieving exploits. After committing several thefts from houses in Nepean Sea road he was caught, convicted and sentenced to a fresh term of six years' imprisonment. All the stolen property was recovered from a Bohra receiver, who worked with Tyebali. In September of the same year information was received from the Director of Criminal Intelligence, Delhi, that three valuable Persian manuscripts had been stolen from the library of Nawab Sir Salar Jung Bahadur at Hyderabad. After a lengthy inquiry the Bombay police traced one of the manuscripts, a *Shahnama*, with illuminated headings and illustrations in colours and gold, which was declared by experts to be an artistic treasure of immense value. A chance remark furnished a clue to the whereabouts of the manuscript, which was in due course returned to its owner in Hyderabad.

Anonymous communications are exceedingly common in India, and as a rule it is practically impossible to trace their authorship. A case of this type, which presented unusual features, was successfully investigated by the police in 1915. For more than two years a series of objectionable and defamatory postcards and letters had been received by high officials, prominent Indians, and clubs. Any event of public interest during that period resulted in a shower of these typed communications, which were always very scurrilous and occasionally flagrantly indecent. They were addressed not only to residents of Bombay, but to officials in other parts of India also, to the Governor, the Viceroy and even to members of the Royal Family in England. The C. I. D. had been able to establish the fact that all the cards and letters were typed on a single machine of a particular and well-known make; and having done that, they proceeded, with the approval of the postal authorities, to subject all the postcards received in the General Post Office to close scrutiny throughout a period of several weeks. At length their patience was rewarded. A card was found, which on careful scrutiny was seen to have been typed on the missing machine, and as it was an ordinary and *bona fide* business communication it was not difficult to locate the machine. It proved to be the property of a well-known Indian merchant, and further inquiry rendered it certain that he was the author of the anonymous cards. He was therefore arrested and released on bail. While the Police were collecting further evidence to support the charge against him, the accused, who had many influential friends, confessed his guilt to one of them and asked his advice. The friend advised him to make a clean breast of the whole matter to the Commissioner of Police and throw himself on his mercy. This he agreed at the moment, but in the end failed, to do and a few days later, while ostensibly endeavouring to light a gas-stove with a bottle of methylated spirit, he was so severely burned about the body that he died in a few hours. The case caused some commotion in the community, to which the accused belonged, and the Commissioner was urged to refrain at the inquest on the deceased from any allusion to the criminal inquiry into the authorship of the postcards. But this the Commissioner refused to do, in view of the wild rumours about the case which were being spread about the City, some of which placed the police in a false and undesirable position. It was doubtless satisfactory to the friends of the deceased that the Coroner's jury found themselves able to pronounce a verdict of accidental death. It only remains to add that after the arrest of the accused the plague of anonymous postcards entirely ceased.

The criminal record of these years would be incomplete without a reference to the collapse in 1913 of a number of Indian banks. The most notable of all, the Indian Specie Bank, was never made the subject of a criminal investigation, though the apathy of its Directors was unquestionable, and its manager, who had set out to "corner" silver against the Indian Government with the monies of the bank's depositors, found it desirable, when the crash came, to die suddenly at Bandora. Orders were issued by the Bombay Government to the Police to investigate the transactions of several lesser banks and bring the guilty to trial; and accordingly a protracted and intricate inquiry was commenced by Inspector Morris of the C.I.D. into the accounts and balance-sheets of the Credit Bank, the Bombay Banking Company and the Cosmopolitan Bank. In the case of the first-named bank, charges of criminal breach of trust and falsification of accounts were proved against the manager, who was sentenced in 1914 to ten years' rigorous imprisonment, while the manager of the Bombay Banking Company and his nephew were likewise convicted of criminal breach of trust and cheating and sentenced to varying terms of imprisonment with hard labour. In the third case the police proved clearly that the bank was not a bank at all, and had neither funds, business nor influence; but the manager and the "bank's" broker, who were charged by the police with cheating, were eventually discharged by the trying magistrate. These bank-failures were not confined to Bombay, but took place in other Provinces also, notably in the Punjab. When the collapse commenced, an attempt was made to draw some of the European-managed banks into the vortex, with the object of showing that the failures were due rather to general economic conditions than to bad management. The attempt failed; for the Scotchmen, who form ninety per cent of the European banking community in India, were too cautious and too solidly entrenched to succumb to any artificial panic, and despite the assertion of some Indian politicians that the European-managed banks, by withholding assistance from these mushroom Indian concerns, had deliberately precipitated the crisis, the general conclusion was that the failures were primarily due to careless or fraudulent management. This view found confirmation in the verdicts delivered in the Courts.

The collapse of at least one bank was due to the uncontrolled habit of speculation which has always distinguished the City of Bombay. Few persons now remain who can remember the famous Share Mania of the early 'sixties: but the spirit of gambling which underlay that colossal financial fiasco is still alive and manifests itself from time to time in wild speculation in the cotton and share markets. The abnormal readiness of the average Indian to follow the lead of any man of outstanding personality, and the ease with which credit is obtained and renewed in Indian circles only serve to aggravate the evil. The suicide of Mr. Dwarkadas Dharamsey, a leading Bhattia mill-agent and merchant, in September, 1909, provided an example of the latitude allowed to one whose financial position had for several years been very unsound. Dwarkadas Dharamsey was a man of great mental capacity, but devoid of scruple. He occupied a leading position in the mercantile and social world, was well-known on the race-course as an owner of horses, was a member of the Municipal Corporation and of the Board of the Improvement Trust, and had been appointed Sheriff of Bombay two or three years before his death. Yet in the very heyday of his prosperity he was spending more than he possessed, staving off importunate demands by all manner of temporary expedients, and juggling with the funds of the mills of which he was director and agent. Faced at last with almost complete insolvency and unable to raise further funds, he shot himself with a revolver at his house in the Fort. He left a kind of confession behind him in which he explained the reason for his action and referred in ambiguous language to some greater crime that he had committed. Though various conjectures were made as to the nature of this act, no definite solution was ever forthcoming. His secret died with him. Immediately after his death, the police discovered that the operatives of his four mills had not been paid their wages for two months, and owing to the closing of the mills they were left stranded and unemployed. With the assistance of Mr. R. D. Sethna, the Official Receiver, the Commissioner was able to get the mill-hands' wages treated as a first charge on the estate of the deceased, and within a short time the wages due to the men were liquidated under Mr. Sethna's orders.

On several occasions Indian constables distinguished themselves by acts of bravery and examples of professional acumen. The detection of a burglary in the showroom of an English firm was due entirely to the action of a Hindu constable, who noticed on a piece of furniture the mark of a foot possessing certain peculiarities, which he remembered having seen before in the foot of an ex-convict. Another Hindu constable grappled with a European who had stabbed a townsman, and though severely wounded in the stomach and bleeding profusely, managed to pursue the offender and hold him down till help came. On three other occasions Indian constables sustained severe wounds, when grappling single-handed with armed Pathans and others, and on each occasion they clung to the prisoner until his arrest was secured. Several instances occurred of women and children being saved from drowning, and in two cases the men were rewarded with the bronze medal of the Royal Humane Society. The action of a young Hindu constable, who had been only three months in the force, deserves more detailed description. About 3 a. m. one morning in August, 1912, a Punjab Muhammadan murdered his comrade in a room in Bapty road. The murder was not discovered till some time afterwards. At 4 a. m. the constable on duty at the junction of Falkland and Foras roads saw a man hurrying in a suspicious manner through the shadows towards Gilder street. He stopped and questioned him; and, his suspicions being aroused, decided to search the man. The fugitive offered the constable a bribe of Rs. 5, Rs. 10 and finally Rs. 30 to let him go; but the constable arrested him and marched him to the Nagpada police station, where a report of the murder had by that time been received. It was then found that the arrested fugitive was the murderer, and that the money with which he had tried to bribe the constable was stained with blood and formed part of the sum which he had stolen from his victim. Further investigation proved beyond doubt that the murdered man had himself stolen the money from an Englishman in Mussoorie. A unique case, in which an accused asked permission of the Magistrate to pay a reward to the constable who arrested him, occurred in 1914. The prisoner, on being questioned, explained that, owing to his timely arrest, he had managed to retain possession of a sum of money, of which he would certainly have been robbed by the disorderly persons with whom he was consorting at the time constable locked him up.

Among the special events of these years which imposed extra work for the time being on the Police were the Nasik murder and conspiracy trials in the High Court in 1910, the visit of Lord Minto in 1909, the arrival of Lord Hardinge and the visit of the ex-German Crown Prince in 1910, and the arrival of Lord Chelmsford in 1916. For the first time on record, the Mounted Police under their European officers were permitted to form part of the escort both of Lord Minto and the German Crown Prince, and, riding grey Arabs in their handsome full-dress uniform, they provided not the least showy part of the spectacle. These Viceregal progresses from the railway terminus or the Apollo Bandar to Malabar Hill had changed in character since the beginning of the twentieth century. Formerly the route chosen for the arrival of a new Viceroy or the departure of his predecessor lay as a matter of course through Kalbadevi road and Bhendy Bazaar, and thence by way of Grant road, or later Sandhurst road, to Chaupati and Walkeshwar. No particular precautions were taken, for none were deemed necessary; the people were well-disposed and always ready to welcome the King's representative as he was driven through the heart of the Indian quarters. But as the anarchical and revolutionary movement spread and attempts were made upon the lives even of Viceroys, the old route through the city was, except for very special reasons, gradually abandoned, and the incoming and departing potentates were escorted along the safer route of Queen's road. The distance of this thoroughfare from the heart of the City, and the growing nonchalance of the majority of the inhabitants in regard to Viceregal appearances in public, were naturally responsible for an absence of sight-seers on the processional route, and at times there were few persons to be seen except the foot-police lining the sides of the road. On the occasion of Lord Chelmsford's arrival in

April, 1916, one of the Superintendents, through whose division a portion of the route passed, determined to keep up appearances of loyal welcome, by collecting the necessary crowd at Sandhurst Bridge and instructing them beforehand in the art of hand-clapping and other manifestations of popular satisfaction. As it was obviously impossible to impress respectable householders and others for this duty, the sectional officers were instructed to shepherd their bad characters of both sexes to the fixed point, after arranging that they all donned clean clothes and were paid 2 annas apiece for their trouble. The plan worked well. As the new Viceroy's carriage swept out of Queen's road on to the bridge, the signal was given and a hearty burst of hand-clapping, punctured with cries of *shabash*, rose from the little crowd of disreputables at the corner. No one knew who they were, except the police who had hunted them out of their haunts a few hours previously: and the Viceroy was doubtless gratified at this signal expression of welcome. When the last of the escort had passed, the unfortunates were taken back to their quarter and there set free to resume their ordinary and less harmless avocations.

There was no need of artificial welcomes of this character when Their Majesties visited Bombay in 1911, or at their final departure in 1912. They drove through the heart of the City ; and both in the wide thoroughfares of the European business-quarter and in the narrower streets of the Indian city they were affectionately greeted and welcomed by thousands of their subjects of all castes and creeds. Their progress was, indeed, a triumph. The choice of the route had not been settled without some doubt and misgiving. The authorities in England declared that the royal procession must not pass along any road of less than a certain width: the Commissioner of Police pointed out that this restriction would entirely debar Their Majesties from entering the City north of Carnac road. The restriction was therefore waived, on condition that the Police adopted all possible measures to render the route completely secure. This by no means easy task was achieved by the C. I. D. and the divisional police, of whom the former spent the three months preceding the Royal Visit in mapping out the houses on the route, making themselves acquainted with all the inmates, posting plain-clothes men and agents in the upper-storeys, and keeping a daily register of arrivals and departures. In one or two cases the divisional police, whose duties lay in holding the route and directing traffic, imposed even stricter conditions than the C. I. D., as the following incident proves. Three or four days before Their Majesties' arrival, an elderly Muhammadan woman of the lower class visited the Head Police Office and asked for an interview with the Commissioner. Her request was granted; and on being shown in, she informed the Commissioner that she occupied a room in the upper-storey of a house near the junction of Sandhurst and Parel roads, and that she desired permission to look out of her window at the royal procession. "But" said the Commissioner, "you need no permission for that." "Yes, Huzur, I do", she answered; "the section-wala (*i. e.* the officer in charge of a police-station) says that unless I obtain a permit I must keep my window shut on the day". It was clearly useless to argue with the old lady, who was honestly bent upon obtaining *darshan* of the *Padshah*. The Commissioner, therefore, wrote out the following pass in his own hand, signed it, and sent her away satisfied :—

"To all Police Officers and those whom it may concern.

> This is to certify that Aminabai, living in House No. .... street, second floor, is hereby granted permission to look out of her own window at His Majesty the King-Emperor, on the occasion of the Royal Progress through Bombay on December 2nd. 1911.
>
> S. M. Edwardes,
> *Commissioner of Police.*"

As an additional precaution the Commissioner of Police asked the Bombay Government to invest him with special magisterial powers, which would enable him to deal summarily with persons of bad character, whose liberty it might be necessary to curtail during the period of the Royal Visit. The request having been granted, the Commissioner proceeded to remand to jail the majority of the well-known hooligans and bad characters, to the number of 400. Fully another three hundred persons with guilty consciences decided to leave Bombay for a holiday up-country, in the belief that they would be sent to jail if they stayed in the City. In this way the City was cleared of seven or eight hundred of its worst characters, and the daily crime returns subsequently proved that the action thus taken produced a very marked diminution of crime during the period of the Royal Visit. Moreover, respectable townspeople, learning of the incarceration of the criminal classes, were able to leave their houses freely at night to visit the illuminations, without fear of burglaries occurring in their absence or of having their pockets picked in the crowd. Political offenders, who usually belonged to a higher stratum of society, were treated differently. In one or two cases they were remanded to jail for treatment as first-class misdemeanants: but the majority were given the option of spending a fortnight in some place chosen by themselves, the police of that place being warned of their arrival and of the need of keeping them under surveillance. In one instance a *détenu* asked to be allowed to visit Ceylon, which he had never seen, and he was accordingly sent there in company with a plain-clothes officer of the C. I. D., who duly escorted him back again at the end of fifteen days. The entire absence of any protest on the part of the public or the Indian press against the Commissioner's action shows that the powers were wielded cautiously and that special measures of this kind were generally accepted as appropriate to the occasion. The wholesale disappearance for the time being of the criminal and hooligan element certainly contributed to the peaceful and orderly progress of the Visit, and produced an immediate and marked decline of crime, which enabled the police to concentrate all their attention on the special arrangements for the functions held during Their Majesties' stay.

Both before and during the Royal Visit, the Police received much help from the public. There was scarcely a householder who did not willingly undertake to carry out the suggestions of the police, and a large number of people, drawn from various classes and communities, volunteered to serve as special constables during the Visit. As to the manner in which the police force itself performed its heavy work, it will suffice to quote the words of the Governor-in-Council, who was "commanded to express to the Police of the City of Bombay His Imperial Majesty's 'entire satisfaction with the admirable police arrangements made during His Imperial Majesty's recent visit to Bombay and with the manner in which they were carried out'". In recognition of the exemplary performance of heavy additional duties, all ranks of the force, from inspectors downwards, received a special bonus, equivalent to ten days' pay. Four Superintendents and three Inspectors received the medal of the Royal Victorian Order from the King-Emperor himself.

The subject of cotton-fires at the Colaba Green was revived by the disastrous epidemic of fires in the cold weather of 1913-14. As previously mentioned, a special committee was appointed by Government, with the Commissioner of Police as chairman, to enquire into the origin of the fires and suggest precautions for the future. The report of this committee, which found that the weight of evidence pointed to wholesale incendiarism, was submitted only a few weeks before the outbreak of War in 1914, and consequently received early burial in the records of the Secretariat. The deductions of the Committee were strengthened to some extent by the inquiries carried out by the C. I. D. during 1914. A thorough examination of the books of various companies established beyond a shadow of doubt that large fortunes had been made over the fires by persons in the cotton trade, as a result of fraudulent dealing, mixing and classification of cotton. This system of dishonesty had been facilitated by slack methods of insurance, which in turn were rendered profitable by clever underwriting. It is doubtful whether these little 'idiosyncrasies' of the Bombay cotton market will ever be wholly eradicated.

It is possible that long after the details of the reorganization of the police force have passed into oblivion, Mr. Edwardes' tenure of office will be remembered for the abolition of the dangerous and rowdy side of the annual Muharram celebration. At the time he was appointed Commissioner, the Muharram, which had been a cause of excitement and anxiety from the days of Forjett, had degenerated into an annual scandal and become a menace to the peace of the city. No respectable Musalman took part in the annual procession of *tabuts*, nor would permit his family to visit the *tazias* and *tabuts* during the ten days of the festival, for fear of insult and annoyance from the *badmashes* and hooligans, who chose the sites of the *tabuts* in the various *mohollas* as their gathering-ground. The cost of building and decorating each *tazia* and *tabut* was defrayed by a public subscription, which had degenerated into pure and simple blackmail, levied by the less respectable denizens of each *moholla* upon the general public. The Marwadi and other Hindu merchants suffered particularly from this practice; at times they were threatened with physical injury if they did not subscribe; on other occasions the collecting-party, composed of four or five Muhammadan roughs, would visit the shops of the Jain merchants, carrying a dead rat, and threaten to drop it into the heaps of grain and sugar if the shop-owner did not forthwith hand out a fair sum. By the exercise of pressure and threats, some *mohollas* contrived to raise comparatively large sums, aggregating several hundred rupees, and as only a fractional portion of this money was required to defray the cost of the *tabut* and the paraphernalia of the final procession, the balance was devoted to the support of the hooligans of the *mohollas* during the following few months. Attached to each *tabut*, and accompanying it whenever it was carried out in procession, was a *toli* or band of attendants, usually varying in numbers from 50 to 200 and composed of the riff-raff of the lower quarters. In some cases these *tolis* had been gradually allowed to assume a gigantic size, as for example that of the Julhai weavers of Ripon road (Madanpura), which comprised from two to three thousand men, all armed with *lathis* tipped with brass or lead. Similarly the notorious Rangari *moholla* (Abdul Rehman street), Halai Memon *moholla*, Kolsa *moholla* and Chuna Batti *moholla*, could count upon turning out several thousand followers, armed with sticks and staves, who could be trusted to render a good account of themselves if there was a breach of the public peace.

The time-honoured sectarian enmity between Sunni and Shia usually showed itself by the second day of the festival, in the form of insults hurled at the Bohras (Shias) by the Sunni rag-tag and bobtail in the various streets occupied by the former. The most notorious of these centres of disturbance was Doctor Street, which debouched into Grant road opposite Sulliman *chauki*; but none of the Bohra quarters were safe from disturbance; and year after year Bohra merchants had to leave Bombay during the festival, or had to secure special protection, and even had to disguise their women in male attire, in the hope of thereby minimising the chance of insult by the lower-class Sunnis. Muharram rioting, which had become much too frequent during the first decade of this century, usually commenced with a fracas of some sort between Sunnis and Bohras, in which the former were generally the aggressors; and when the Police intervened to restore order, the mob on one pretext or another declared war against them with the inevitable result. The Sunni hooligans would never have reached the pitch of insolence which marked their behaviour in 1910, had they not felt assured that they had the support of the leading Sunnis residing in the *mohollas,* many of whom, though comparatively wealthy, were almost illiterate and totally uncultured; and the latter in turn were prompted to foster the more rowdy and disreputable aspects of the festival by the belief that the Moslem community thereby acquired more importance, even though of a sinister character, in the eyes of Government, and that the possibility of disturbance could be occasionally used as a lever to secure consideration or concessions in other directions.

This belief was partly confirmed by the attitude of the authorities, who persisted in attaching undue weight to the religious character of the festival,—a character which had practically ceased to have any influence on the celebrants, and in accordance with the time-honoured principle of strict religious neutrality showed great reluctance to impose any restrictions upon the celebration. The Police, who in times of disturbance often reaped a fair harvest of tips and presents from timorous towns-people who desired protection from mob-violence, and who also discovered in the aftermath of rioting an easy means of paying off old scores, had never troubled to explain to Government the precise character and danger of the annual Muharram. The old doctrine of "the safety-valve" was still in favour, with the result that during the concluding days of the festival Bombay used to witness the spectacle of police officers of the upper ranks urging the most uncompromising rascals to lift the *tabuts* and form the processions, regardless of the fact that at any other season of the year they would not have hesitated to lock up most of these disreputables at sight. In short, under the cloak of religion, the worst elements in the bazaar were permitted to burst their bounds for ten days and flow over the central portion of the City in a current of excessive turbulence, to terrorize the peaceful householder and to play intolerable mischief in the streets. If the leaders and wire-pullers decided that there should be a disturbance, culminating in a conflict with the police, all they had to do was to pass the order to the various *mohollas* not to "lift" their *tabuts* on the tenth day and to the Bara Imam shrine in Khoja street not to send out the *sandal*-procession on the ninth night. This latter procession was, so to speak, the barometer of the Muharram, and its non-appearance in the streets invariably indicated storm. Once it had been decided not to "lift" the *tabuts*, the huge *tolis*, which should have accompanied them to their final immersion in the sea, were let loose in the streets with nothing to do, and a breach of the peace was rendered practically inevitable. When this point was reached on the last day, it was customary for the Afghans and Pathans, residing in the B division, to collect in groups in the lanes behind Parel road (Bhendy Bazar), and at the right moment to commence looting and setting fire to shops. In the Muharram riots of 1908 it was these people who set fire to a shop on Parel road and threw a Hindu constable into the middle of the flames. The only unobjectionable feature of the old Muharram was the *Waaz* or religious discourse, which was delivered nightly in each of the leading *mohollas* by a chosen *Maulvi* or *Mulla.* Unfortunately these were very little patronized by the hooligans and damaged characters, who composed the *tolis* and monopolized the celebration of the festival in the streets.

Mr. Edwardes' first Muharram in 1910 ended without an actual breach of the peace: but the behaviour of the *mohollas* was so insolent, and the license and obscenity displayed by the mob were so intolerable, particularly in the Bohra quarter of the C division, that he determined to impose restrictions at the Muharram of January, 1911. Accordingly in December, 1910, he issued a notification closing Doctor Street and the neighbouring lanes running parallel with it to all processionists throughout the period of the festival, and from the first night he placed a strong cordon of police round the prohibited area, to prevent any attempt by the mob to break the order. Practically the whole police force was on continuous duty for ten days and nights in the streets, and commissariat arrangements for both European and Indian police had to be made on the spot. Though no serious trouble occurred during the first few days of the festival, there were several indications of trouble brewing, and the Commissioner therefore arranged with Brigadier-General John Swann to hold garrison troops in readiness. On the tenth night or *Katal-ki-rat* a serious disturbance broke out in Bhendy Bazar about 3 a. m., in connexion with the procession of the Rangari *mohulla tabut*. Free fighting between the processionists and the mob from other *mohullas* took place all the way from Grant road to Pydhoni, and it was due solely to the efforts of Mr. Vincent, the Deputy Commissioner, and a handful of police who were escorting the procession, that the *tabut* was eventually brought back to its resting-place. The mob by this time had tasted blood and displayed so truculent an attitude that the Commissioner decided to telephone for the troops and picket them throughout the danger zone. By 4 a. m. on January 12th the troops had taken their places, and the mob, for the moment deeming discretion the better part of valour, melted away in the darkness. About 5 p. m., however, in the afternoon of the same day, the mob, which declined to carry out the *tabuts* in procession, collected on Parel road and Memonwada road and commenced stoning the troops and police. They also stopped all traffic, stoned tram-cars and private carriages, and roughly handled several harmless pedestrians. The police made several charges upon them from Pydhoni, but were unable permanently to disperse the rioters. At length the Commissioner, seeing that the two mobs refused to disperse and were practically out of hand, and that the Pathans were on the point of breaking loose, called Rao Bahadur Chunilal H. Setalwad, one of the Presidency Magistrates, who was on duty at Sulliman Chauki, and asked him to give the order to the troops (the Warwickshire Regiment) picketed at Pydhoni to fire on the mob. The order was given at once and the rioting ceased. [1]

Like Napoleon's famous "whiff of grapeshot", the firing of the Warwicks may be said to have blown the old Muharram into the limboof oblivion. From that date, January 1911, the processional part of the Muharram, with its *tolis*, its blackmail, its terrorism and its obscenities, ceased to exist and has not up to the present 1922 been revived. Before the succeeding Muharram drew near, the Commissioner had framed new rules for the celebration, of which the deposit by *tabut*-license holders of ample security for good behaviour and a complete revision of the processional route for each *tabut* were two of the main features. He had also contrived to persuade the leaders of the various Muhammadan sections and *mohollas* that the orgiastic method of celebrating the festival was an anachronism, not countenanced by Islamic teaching and gravely injurious to the City. In thus securing the obliteration of the customs and practices, which for more than fifty years had been responsible for periodical outbreaks of disorder, the Commissioner was greatly assisted by some of the leading men of the Sunni *jamats*, of whom the most conspicuous and most helpful was Sirdar Saheb Sulliman Cassum Haji Mitha, C. I. E., of Kolsa *Moholla*. He led the way at succeeding Muharrams in popularizing the *waaz* or nightly religious discourses and in spending upon them, and upon illuminations and charitable distribution of food to the poorer classes, the money which was formerly wasted on irreverent and turbulent

1. A full and detailed report of the disturbance is given in Mr. Edwardes' letter to Government, No. 545 C. of January 20th. 1911, printed below as an Appendix.

processions. For this fundamental change in the character of the festival none perhaps were more grateful than the *Maulvis* and *Mullas* who presided over the *waaz*; for with the disappearance of the *tolis* and their paraphernalia their audiences were enormously increased. But respectable Moslems and the general public also breathed a sigh of relief, on realizing that the long-standing annual menace to law and order had been exorcised. In December, 1914, on the conclusion of the fourth Muharram celebrated in the new manner, the Bombay Government wrote to Mr. Edwardes, expressing their thanks for his unremitting efforts and skilful management of the festival. "The result", they remarked, "is in large measure due to the excellent relations which you established between the Muhammadan leaders and yourself, thus rendering it possible to relegate to the past the disreputable ceremonies which used to disfigure the Muharram. It is now possible to regard the new regulations as having become permanently established".

Such, very briefly, is the history of the purification of the Bombay Muharram. The old days, when the police were on continuous duty for ten days and nights, when the Bohras were subjected to volleys of the vilest and most obscene abuse and to open assault, when the lowest and most turbulent portion of the population was permitted to take charge of the central portion of the city, and when rioting with its complement of drastic repression was liable to recur in any year—those days have passed, and one hopes that a weak administration will never permit them to recur. The present puritanical and more reverent method of celebration was firmly established during Mr. Edwardes' Commissionership with the help and approval of leading Muhammadans, who realized at length that the annual orgy in the streets was a disgrace to Islam.

It remains only to notice the effect upon the police of the outbreak of the Great War in August, 1914. The day after War was declared, local shopkeepers, particularly the dealers in foodstuffs, commenced to raise their prices to famine level, and large numbers of the poorer classes appealed to the police for assistance. Government having decided to appoint a food-price committee, the Commissioner ordered a *battaki* to be beaten throughout the City for three days; several shopkeepers who were disposed to be recalcitrant were called up to the Head Police Office and warned; and in several cases constables were posted at shops to see that prices were not unduly raised. Excess amounts received by shop-keepers from mill-hands and others were in many cases recovered and paid back to the purchasers, and a series of judiciously-fabricated reports were spread by chosen agents, describing the imaginary fate which had overtaken certain shopkeepers, who had extorted fancy prices from the public. Somewhat similar action was taken with excellent effect in the case of retail-dealers, who refused to accept currency-notes of small denominations from the poorer classes. Within a few days these measures produced the required effect, and trade again became normal. The police were on constant duty day and night at the Government Dockyard, at the various military camps erected for the Indian Expeditionary Force, and during the economic disturbance in the early days of the War at the banks and Currency Office. They assisted the military authorities to find Dhobis, Bhistis and other camp-followers for enrolment, they traced absentee followers and native seamen, and during the heavy rain-storms of October, 1914, they found accommodation in permanent buildings for the troops under canvas. They took charge of coal-stacks for the Director, R. I. M., and did much extra duty at the Wadi Bandar railway goods-sheds. They displayed great tact in their management of the crowds which used to collect in the streets to hear the special editions of the vernacular newspapers read out during the early months of the War; and during the aeroplane scare, they were equally successful in dealing with the mobs which used to scan the skies for airships. While the *Emden* was seizing vessels in the Bay of Bengal and bombarding Madras, there was again a scare in the City and some of the more timorous merchants, taking their cash and jewellery with them, fled to their homes in Native States, where in several cases the local police kindly relieved them of most of their valuables. Others, equally timorous but more reasonable, applied to the Police Commissioner for advice, and were satisfied with his assurance that if it should become necessary to vacate Bombay, he would give them ample warning beforehand. Trusting to this promise, many Hindu merchants remained in the City, who would otherwise have fled.

During the movement of the Expeditionary Forces, the scenes in certain quarters of the bazar, which were heavily patronized by soldiers and sailors, both European and Indian, beggared description. The Japanese quarter appeared to offer special attractions to fighting-men of Mongolian type, and the divisional police had a hard task to settle disputes and maintain order in these areas. In the mill-district there was unrest for some little time; but this was at length discounted by the labours of three Hindu gentlemen, Messrs. H. A. Talcherkar, S. K. Bole, and K. R. Koregaonkar, who volunteered their services as intermediaries between the Police Commissioner and the industrial population, and by means of lectures on the war, social gatherings and so forth, helped to keep the police in touch with popular feeling and to minimise panic. Very arduous work fell upon the Harbour police in connexion with the patrol of the various bandars and wharves, the boarding of all vessels entering the harbour, and the many miscellaneous and emergent requisitions entailed by war conditions. The old police launch which at its best was never very seaworthy, broke down under the strain and had to be docked for repairs to her machinery; but the Harbour police continued to carry on their duties by borrowing launches from other departments. The desertion of lascar crews at the beginning of the submarine scare caused much trouble to the Shipping Master and to the steamship-companies, and on several occasions *serangs* and other Indian seamen were brought to the Head Police Office to have their apprehensions allayed. When Turkey entered the war, the Divisional police took a census and compiled a register of all Turkish subjects in the City, excluding certain wealthy Arabs of the upper class, who were visited by Muhammadan police officers specially deputed for this duty by the Commissioner.

The bulk of the confidential war work fell naturally upon the Criminal Investigation Department. Before the organization of the Postal Censor's office, and in some cases also afterwards, the department scrutinized letters addressed to enemy subjects; it studied closely the daily and weekly newspapers in all languages, and prepared a daily report for the military authorities on the publication of war-news; it carried out requests for information and assistance from the Brigade Office, the Customs Department, and the Controller of Hostile Trading Concerns. It prepared lists for Government of hostile, allied and neutral foreigners resident in Bombay; it mustered all German and Austrian males, numbering respectively 189 and 37, at the Head Police Office, confiscated their fire-arms, and eventually dispatched them under arrest to the Ahmadnagar Detention Camp, whither were also sent many enemy foreigners subsequently removed from enemy ships in the harbour. It also kept under surveillance a certain number of persons who were permitted to remain on parole in Bombay; it kept under observation and deported a large number of transfrontier Pathans and tribesmen, under special powers granted for this purpose to the Commissioner; it arrested the officers and crew of a captured Turkish vessel and placed them in detention, and deported many Turkish subjects to Jeddah. The department also housed and fed for two months two hundred and sixty Chinese, who were removed from German prize vessels. One of the more amusing features of their arrival was the disgust shown by the Muhammadan police-officer, told off to arrange for their supply of food, when they begged him in a body to buy up all the pork he could find in the bazaar. Military prisoners from Mesopotamia were taken over and placed in charge of the proper authorities; constant inquiries were made about firms suspected of trading with the enemy; and from the end of 1915 the department had to organize a system of passes for all persons desiring to land at Basra or Mohammerah.

The process of clearing Bombay of hostile aliens of both sexes was finally completed in 1915. Among them were six ladies, a few children, one or two Jesuit priests, and eighteen prostitutes, who were sent to Calcutta for repatriation to Holland by the S. S. *Golconda*. This party left Bombay by special train, the respectable women and children being placed in the front carriages, the priests and the police-escort in the centre, and the unfortunate denizens of the brothels in the rear-compartments. The moment of departure was enlivened by a gentleman, belonging to the priestly class of a well-known community, who had been keeping one of the Austrian harlots. He came to see the lady off and burst into floods of tears and loud groans, as the train steamed out of the station. One of the most ticklish duties entrusted to the police occurred during the Muharram of 1915. A regiment composed of north-country Muhammadans was on the point of embarking for Mesopotamia, when one of the men murdered their English major. He was court-martialled without delay and sentenced to be hanged; and the military authorities, who handed him over to the police pending his execution, were very anxious that his punishment should be witnessed by the rest of the regiment. There was a general undercurrent of unrest at the time in the Muhammadan quarter, owing to sympathy with Turkey, and the Muharram festival was in progress. Any undue publicity given to the execution, and the overt movement of troops through the City, might have brought about an outbreak. Arrangements were therefore made by the Police to hang the culprit at the Byculla jail before daybreak and to march the regiment to the spot by a circuitous route, with a British regiment in attendance to prevent any attempt at mutiny. The execution was carried out without a hitch, and the regiment was back at its temporary quarters in the docks before the City was properly awake.

In conclusion it may be added that the whole police force, and the clerical staff of the Commissioner, subscribed one day's pay apiece to the Bombay Presidency Branch of the Imperial War Relief Fund. This sum was augmented to a total of Rs. 15,000 by subscriptions received by the Commissioner from a motley assortment of local characters, among whom may be mentioned the leading Hindu dancing-girls, the Sadhus and Bairagis in Bai Jankibai's *dharamshala*, the local Pathans working in the Docks, the Sidis or African Muhammadans, the Persian Zoroastrians or Iranis, who are mostly tea-shop keepers, and a Parsi amateur theatrical company. It says something for the good relations subsisting between the police and the general public that classes such as these voluntarily offered their contributions as soon as the general appeal for funds was issued under the auspices of Lord Willingdon, the Governor.

In two respects the Commissioner's *régime* was fortunate. He had an excellent and very hardworking clerical staff; and the relations between the Magistracy and the Police were uniformly cordial. Shortly after Mr. Edwardes joined the appointment in 1909, the old head-clerk, Mr. Ramchandra Dharadhar, retired, and his place was taken by Mr. Vinayakrao Dinanath, whose early service dated back to the days of Sir Frank Souter. Under him and the second clerk, Mr. Chhaganlal M.

Tijoriwala, I. S. O., who has since succeeded to the head-clerk's post with the title of "Superintendent of the Commissioner's office," an immense volume of correspondence was dealt with, which was often of so urgent a character that the staff was obliged to work on Sundays and to give up the public and sectional holidays allowed to all departments of Government.

Throughout this period the appointment of Chief Presidency Magistrate was held by Mr. A. H. S. Aston, whose transparent honesty of thought and purpose would have been an asset to any Bench; and he was ably seconded by Rao Bahadur Chunilal H. Setalwad, C. I. E., Mr. Oliveira, and Mr. Gulamhussein R. Khairaz. Mr. Setalwad combined with wide legal experience a valuable knowledge of the customs and idiosyncrasies of the many classes resident in Bombay, and in seasons of unrest and disturbance he was among the first to offer his services to the Police Commissioner towards the restoration of order. While he and his colleagues gave the police every support from the Bench, they never hesitated to inform the Commissioner personally of cases in which, in their opinion, the subordinate police had acted in error or exceeded their powers—a course of action which was most helpful to the head of the police force.

By the end of 1915 the strain of nearly seven years' work and the additional burden imposed by war conditions had told so heavily upon Mr. Edwardes' health that he asked the Bombay Government to transfer him to another appointment. He was offered and accepted the post of Municipal Commissioner, and bade a final adieu to the Police force on April 15th, 1916. But he was not destined to serve long in the Municipality. An old pulmonary complaint, which was seriously aggravated by the constant strain of police duty, developed so rapidly that he was obliged to take furlough to England in the following October and eventually to retire from the service on medical certificate in April, 1918. A few months after his final retirement, the Governor of Bombay, Lord Willingdon, unveiled at the Head Police Office a marble bust of the ex-Commissioner, which, in the words engraved on the pedestal, was "erected by subscriptions from all ranks of the Bombay City Police in appreciation of many and valued services rendered to the Force".

APPENDIX

MR. EDWARDES' REPORT ON THE FINAL MOHARRAM RIOT OF 1911 AND THE BOMBAY GOVERNMENT'S ORDER THEREON

No. 1431

Bombay Castle, 8th March, 1911

Disturbances in Bombay during the Moharram of 1911

No. 545—C, dated 20th January, 1911

From—S. M. Edwardes, Esquire, I. C. S.,
Commissioner of Police, Bombay;

To—The Secretary to Government,
Judicial Department, Bombay.

I have the honour to state with regret that a serious outbreak took place in the City on the early morning of the 12th January in connection with the Moharram Tabut procession and that it was followed on the afternoon of the same day by a violent disturbance of such a character that I was forced to send for a magistrate to give an order to the troops, on duty at the scene of disturbance, to fire on the mob. I submit hereunder a full account of the circumstances which rendered this order necessary.

2. The Moharram of 1911 commenced on the 2nd January. As Government are aware, I had with their approval issued a notification, dated 8th December 1910, closing Pakmodia Street, Dhabu Street, Doctor Street, Chimna Butcher Street and Mutton Street to all processionists throughout the Moharram. This order was rendered necessary by the behaviour of the Mahommedan Mohollas at the Moharram of 1910 and by the intolerable rowdiness and obscene license which for the last 6 or 7 years have characterized the progress of the procession through the Shia Borah locality of Doctor Street and neighbouring lanes.

3. The notification was not favourably received by the lower classes who take part in the Bombay Moharram, but was welcomed both by the Shias and respectable Sunnis as a step in the right direction. Till about a week before the first night of the festival it was generally understood that the various Mohollas would not apply for licenses and that they would sulk as they did last year. This in itself constitutes a serious menace to public peace and order, as the non-appearance of the tabuts and tazias in the streets lets loose the gangs or *tolis* (numbering several thousands and composed of the riffraff of the Musalman quarter) which usually accompany the mimic tombs to the water-side. However, after considerable vacillation, the leading Mohollas, Rangari, Kolsa, Chuna Batti and others, held a meeting at which it was decided openly to apply for licenses to me and to celebrate the festival in the usual manner. Shortly after this meeting it transpired that one of those who advocated most strongly the application for licenses and the observance of the police orders regarding Doctor Street was one Badlu, who lives in Madanpura and controls a tabut supported by the Julhai weavers of that locality. It appears that his action was part of a settled policy between himself and the notorious Rangari Moholla, the nature of which will be disclosed a little further on. It also transpired that the Konkani Mahomedan Mohollas were up in arms both against my order and against Rangari Moholla and its leader, Latiff, the tea shop-keeper, and that they found strong sympathisers among the Mohollas of the E division, and Bengalpura, Teli Gali, Bapu Hajam and Kasai Mohollas in the B division. The bone of contention was the closing of Doctor Street. The Konkani Mahomedans declared that the behaviour of the Mohollas at the Moharram of 1910 had obliged the Police Commissioner to take action in regard to Doctor Street, which was perfectly true, and secondly that that behaviour had been dictated and forced upon all the Mohollas in 1910 by Latiff and the Memons of Rangari Moholla, which was equally undeniable. They were incensed to find Latiff now advocating the observance of the festival and obedience to the Police Order, and declared that *they* would not lift their tabuts and would not have anything further to do with Rangari Moholla. Nevertheless, while thus secretly determined not to go out in procession and nursing violent hostility to Rangari Moholla, they declared openly that there was nothing

amiss and applied for tabut licenses as soon as Rangari, Kolsa and Chuna Batti Mohollas applied for theirs.

4. The policy of Badlu and Latiff of Rangari Moholla became apparent as soon as Latiff applied for his tabut-license. He asked me personally to grant the Julhais a pass for the procession. For, finding that there was considerable feeling against him among the Konkanis and the Mohollas who sympathised with them, he foresaw that, unless he commanded a strong following from some other quarter, the Rangari Moholla procession would be rather a poor one. He therefore without doubt arranged with Badlu that if he (Latiff) could squeeze a pass out of the Police, the Julhais were to amalgamate with his Moholla and make a brave display in front of the recalcitrant Mohollas.

I refused absolutely to give a pass, after consulting all persons who were in a position to give an opinion on the point. Government are aware that the Julhais are an extremely illiterate and fanatical population. When once an individual gets influence over them, they will do anything that he asks ; and it has always been the policy of the police to forbid their bringing their tabut out in the ordinary procession and to prevent them coming anywhere south of the Parsi Statue on the *Katal-ki-rat* and the last day. The Julhais can, if they obtain a pass, bring out a *toli* of about 3,000 men, all armed with *lathis*, many of which are knobbed and tipped with brass or iron. I have had something to do with them, in the matter of getting them re-employed after a strike and obtaining their back wages from their employers : and in view of the gratitude which they professed for this help, I decided to send for Badlu myself and explain to him that it was impossible for me to grant them a pass, much as I regretted my inability to do so. Badlu after 20 minutes' talk with me was quite reasonable and undertook not to worry any more about a pass and to keep his following cool. Apparently Latiff and Rangari Moholla were not very pleased at my having checkmated them, and from that moment Latiff began to talk somewhat ambiguously about the possible failure of the procession. Badlu, however, stuck to his promise to me, and the Julhais in a body took their tabut out and immersed it in the usual way in the area north of the Parsi Statue.

5. The next symptom of possible trouble concerned the *ugarání* or collection of funds for the tabut and procession, which each Moholla levies on the general public. Government are possibly not aware that it costs a Moholla anything from Rs. 100 to 400 to erect a Tabut and carry it out, and there are 105 Mohollas in the city which usually do so. The bulk of this money is extorted—there is no other word for it—from Marwadi and Bania merchants, who are threatened with physical injury unless they subscribe liberally. Just prior to the commencement of the Moharram, certain Marwadi merchants came and made a complaint at the Paidhuni Police Station that they were being harassed and assaulted by Bengalpura Moholla. The Divisional Police very properly made an enquiry into the complaint and finding it to be true, sent for the leaders of that Moholla and gave them a strict warning not to extort any more money from Hindu merchants. This was treated as a grievance, and Latiff himself had the impertinence to come to the Head Police Office and complain that "the police were not assisting the collection of funds".

Added to these alleged grievances, rumour was also rife that the Bohras had been openly boasting that they had got Doctor Street closed and that they had won a victory over the Sunnis. I believe there is some foundation for this report, and that some of the lower-class Bohras, who number amongst them several very bad characters, did inflame the minds of individual Sunnis by talking and acting in a very indiscreet manner.

6. Such was the position at the opening of the Moharram on the 2nd January. In view of the notification alluded to above and in order to prevent any attempt to rush Doctor Street, I had to place a permanent cordon round the prohibited area from the first night, consisting of 324 native police and 30 European officers. In addition to this I had strong guards at Paidhuni, Sulliman Chowkey, the J. J. Hospital corner and Nall Bazaar, which were strengthened from the 6th night of the Moharram with pickets of armed police and mounted police. The men on the cordon and at the places mentioned were on practically continuous duty for ten nights and days, a few only being allowed off duty as opportunity offered to get their meals. I bring to the notice of Government that the strain on these men was very great, and that in consequence of the disturbance on the last day I had to

retain them for three days and nights after their duty should in ordinary circumstances have ceased.

7. Nothing of any importance happened on the first night, except a little scuffle at the Shia Imambara on Jail Road, when a Sunni *toli* was passing with music. The care-taker dashed out and abused the *toli*, which retorted by flinging a few stones at the Imambara and playing more loudly than before. This trouble was however allayed and no serious consequences ensued. On the 2nd night (following the first day) nothing of importance occurred, and the same was the case up to the 5th January. On that day I personally interviewed the leaders of the Pathans, Sidis and Panjabis and asked them to warn their respective class-fellows against going out and joining any *toli*. This they promised to do. No Sidis or Panjabis came out: but on the last day when the trouble commenced, the Pathans and Peshawaris were out in considerable force, throwing stones at the tram-cars and the Police, in spite of the fact that Samad Khan, one of the Pathan headmen, tried his best to hold his branch in check.

On the same day (5th January) I received a report from the D division that, according to rumour, the only Mohollas that intended to go out with their tabuts were Rangari, Kolsa and Chuna Batti Mohollas, and that if they actually did go out there would be trouble in Nagpada. Other rumours of an equally disquieting nature were abroad, which obliged the C. I. D. and Inspector Khan Bahadur Shaikh Ibrahim to redouble their efforts to smooth away spurious grievances and bring about a feeling of tranquillity. Nevertheless we hoped for the best and watched the *panjas* and the *pethis* come out on the 5th night (6th January) and pass down Grant Road, without making any serious attempt to break away down Doctor Street.

8. On the 7th night of Moharram (Sunday the 8th January) the Rangari Moholla *toli* and the Halai Memon Moholla *toli* turned out in force at a very late hour. In spite of the Police order that they should be back in their Mohollas by 2 a. m., it was 4 a. m. before they reached home and it was 4-30 a. m. before the Deputy Commissioners and I were able to leave the City. Before they started a reminder was sent to them about the carrying of "lathis" and bludgeons, and, so far as I can gather, out of the two to three thousand persons composing each

toli, a considerable number were unarmed when they left their Mohollas. They wandered out of the B division into the C division, and thence gradually up Khoja Street to Grant Road. When they arrived at Sulliman Chowkey, Superintendent Priestley, who had been with them on their peregrinations for 2 hours and 20 minutes, reported that they had collected sticks on the route and had even torn down and armed themselves with the poles which support the awnings over the shops. As they passed me they appeared to be in a condition of considerable exaltation, and I was able to note the scum of which the *tolis* were composed. There is no question of religion or religious fervour here. The *tolis* are irreligious rascality, let loose for five days and nights to play intolerable mischief in the streets and terrorize the peaceful householder.

On their way out from their Moholla the Rangari *toli* took a new route. Instead of coming direct up Abdul Rehman Street, as it always has done, it turned off into the Koka Bazaar, where many Bohras live and where there is a Bohra mosque, and there it drummed and played and hurled obscene abuse at the Bohras in the same way as it has done in Doctor Street. In fact, it passed the word round that though Doctor Street had been closed by the Police, it had found a new Doctor Street and had checkmated the Commissioner.

9. The action of these two *tolis* produced the inevitable result. Some of the others, who were hesitating about coming out, got their blood up and turned out in great force on the following night (Monday the 9th). They were Kolsa Moholla, Kasai Moholla (the beef-butchers), the Bapty Road Chillichors or hack victoria drivers, and Teli Gali. These *tolis* also were fully armed. We held a consultation as to whether it was advisable to rush in and disarm the crowds; but in view of the enormous size of the *tolis*, and the fact that most of our police were locked up in the cordoned area, and further that any show of force would have inevitably led to a disturbance of a serious character, I let the question of sticks slide and confined the police to urging the *tolis* home as quickly as possible. From the 6th night we had to exercise the greatest caution in order not to precipitate a conflict, and in doing so we were obliged to wink at certain things which with a stronger police force we might have forcibly put down. We

kept Doctor Street and the other streets hermetically closed from the beginning to the end, but this was only achieved by denuding our main posts and a considerable portion of the city of both European and Native police.

Two points deserve notice in connection with the *toli* procession of the 9th January. First, Kasai Moholla on its way home turned into Koka Bazaar, assaulted one or two Bohras, and looted a few shops. On hearing this I drew off my armed police guard at Paidhuni and placed it in Koka Bazaar, and also placed 5 armed native police at each end. Secondly, Teli Moholla took the ominous step of coming out a short distance and then going back to its quarters. This is invariably a dangerous sign; and there is little doubt that Teli Moholla did this as a signal to the Konkani Mohollas, Bengalpura, and the Mohollas of the E division that the Moharram was to be wrecked, partly as a protest against the closing of Doctor Street and partly out of enmity to Rangari Moholla. Once more the C. I. D. and Khan Bahadur Shaikh Ibrahim did their best to smooth away difficulties, and once more we looked forward with slightly diminished hopes to the next day (10th January). When one left for home at 5 a. m. on the 10th January, one could not help feeling that the odds were slightly against our getting through the festival without trouble, but I still hoped that if Rangari, Kolsa and Chuna Batti Mohollas came out properly on the 10th night or *Katal-ki-rat*, the others would lift their tabuts on the last day, and all would be well.

10. On the 9th night (10th January) we exerted all our influence to keep the various Mohollas in a good temper. Mr. Vincent went with his most trusted C. I. D. officers to the E division Mohollas, spoke with the crowd, listened to their *Waaz* or nightly discourse, subscribed to their funds and finally left them apparently happy and determined to carry out their tabuts properly. Meanwhile Mr. Gadney and I visited the B division tabuts, talked with the tabutwallas, and endeavoured to allay the tension, which was obviously spreading through the Musalman quarter. At the four chief Mohollas we visited we were received in friendly style; but I was made to understand secretly that none of them would lift their tabuts unless Rangari Moholla gave the lead, and that the Konkani Mohollas were absolutely obdurate and hostile.

The latter fact was sufficiently proved by the non-appearance of the Bara Imam Sandal procession, which usually starts from Khoja Street on the 9th night. It serves as the barometer of the Moharram and its non-appearance in the streets usually indicates storm. Every form of persuasion was used to make the licensee start out, as soon as the news of his recalcitrance reached me. But to no avail. Whether the licensee was a member of the cabal bent upon creating disturbance or whether he was, as he stated, afraid to move out, I cannot exactly say. But it is tolerably certain that the recalcitrant faction, including Bengalpura and Teli Gali, sent him a secret message that if he dared to leave Khoja Street, he and his processionists would be mobbed and hurt.

In spite of this we persuaded Chuna Batti Moholla to issue, and they were followed by old and new Bengalpura who were playing a double game, and by Kasar Gali and Wadi Bandar, whom Mr. Vincent had screwed up to the starting-point by his diplomatic visit. Nothing of note occurred during this procession of several thousand persons, except that they started late and kept us in the streets till 4-45 a. m.

11. Thus we reached the 10th night or *Katal-ki-rat*, which precedes the last or Immersion Day (January 12th). On the night of the 11th January I reached Paidhuni at 10 p.m. and there met Rao Bahadur Chunilal Setalvad, who had heard conflicting rumours and had offered his services to me in case I required them. We determined to wait there until the processions of the B division began to move out round the City, which should have happened about 11-45 p. m. By midnight the streets were crowded, but there was no sign of a procession. At 12-30 a. m. I received information that Latiff and Rangari Moholla had started out. In order to make quite certain I went down Abdul Rehman Street to find out where they were and give them a lead forward. I could not find them for some time, but finally caught sight of their torches moving down the south end of Koka Bazaar towards Carnac Road, in other words in the opposite direction to which they ought to have been moving. The next thing I heard was that they had turned back, placed their tabut down in its *mándwa* and declined to go any further. Knowing that this in itself spelt trouble, and having been told that unless Rangari Moholla lifted its tabut none of the others would, I sent the divisional police to fetch Latiff, and told him that if he did not take out his tabut in procession along the proper route I would leave no

stone unturned to punish him. Latiff was genuinely afraid and promised to start out again. So at length, about 1-45 a.m., the Rangari Moholla tabut moved up Abdul Rehman Street towards Paidhuni, with drums, band, torches, and a bullock cart containing oil and wood to replenish the torches. On arrival at Paidhuni, Latiff implored police protection for his procession, in view of the anger of Teli Gali, Bengalpura and the Konkani Mohollas. I therefore sent 4 sowars, several foot police and 4 European officers with the procession, while Mr. Vincent and some C. I. D. men undertook to walk ahead and see them safely into the C division limits.

Having thus started Rangari Moholla, I went down to Kolsa Moholla, Chuna Batti and Halai Moholla to get them to start out. Kolsa Moholla had already set forth once, but had retreated on hearing that Rangari Moholla had also done so. After immense delay, caused by these Mohollas making excuses that they had no coolies to carry the tabuts and that their bandsmen had run away, we managed to get all three into one long line containing several thousand persons and brought them out to the junction of Memonwada Road and Bhendy Bazaar. It was now about 3-30 a.m. At the moment that the front ranks turned the corner I looked up Bhendy Bazaar and saw in the far distance the lights and flares of Rangari Moholla returning. Knowing the hereditary animosity between Kolsa and Rangari Mohollas, and believing that if they met face to face in Bhendy Bazaar there would be a free fight, I managed with the help of Khan Bahadur Shaikh Ibrahim and the B division police to push the whole procession into Goghari Moholla, on its way up to the Nall Bazaar and Khoja Street, before Rangari Moholla had had time to get as far south. I sent two European police officers and some native police with the procession to see it safely through the C and E divisions.

Meanwhile I had received information from Mr. Gadney, who was at Sulliman Chowkey, that a very ugly-looking crowd was following behind the Rangari Moholla *toli*; and having got rid of the three other Mohollas, I determined to await the arrival of Rangari Moholla at Paidhuni and see what happened. About 3-45 a.m. it reached me in very sorry plight. It appears that having seen the tabut and *toli* safely into the C division, Mr. Vincent walked by a side street to Nall

Bazaar and escorted it thence to Sulliman Chowkey. By that time the *toli* was being followed by an obviously hostile crowd, whistling and shouting "Huriya, Huriya", the usual signal for disorder. Four more European officers from Sulliman Chowkey and the Doctor Street guard were therefore sent with the procession, while Mr. Vincent and a few C. I. D. officers walked behind the procession and between it and the crowd. Thus they left Sulliman Chowkey. After rounding the J. J. Hospital corner into Bhendy Bazaar the trouble began. The crowd, which was strengthened every minute by swarms of malcontents from the side *galis*, practically mobbed the police and the tabut procession all the way down Bhendy Bazaar. They shouted, whistled and used the filthiest language: they stoned the police and Rangari Moholla unceasingly; they beat the sowars and their horses with *lathis*, bringing one down; they carried on a hand-to-hand conflict as far as Paidhuni. The torch-bearers of Rangari Moholla put down their lights andfled, and the mob threw the lighted wood at the police. The tabut was within an ace of being abandoned when the Police seized the bearers and forced them to carry it on. Latiff was quivering with fear. Several times the European police begged Mr. Vincent to give orders to fire on the mob, which it was increasingly difficult to ward off, and each time Mr. Vincent refused, telling them to use their batons only and force the tabut and procession into the safer lanes of the B division. So they gradually arrived, fighting with the mob the whole way and being continuously stoned. A European officer and 2 native constables had to be sent to hospital to get their wounds dressed. At one point of the route a Pathan ranged himself on the side of the police and did remarkable execution on the mob with a *lathi*.

12. On hearing from Mr. Vincent at Paidhuni what had happened, and seeing that the crowd was increasing round the police station, I decided (*a*) to call for military assistance in picketing the streets and (*b*) to have a baton-charge on the mob. By this time it was quite obvious that the mob was composed of the worst elements in the recalcitrant Konkani Mohollas, Bengalpura and Teli Gali, aided, I believe, by the Kasai Moholla and Babu Hajam Moholla *badmashes*, who had definitely declined to lift their tabut. Since the 6th night I had, with the approval and assistance of General Swann,

quartered 2 companies of the Warwickshire Regiment in the Head Police office as a precautionary measure. For eighty of these I at once telephoned and they arrived within 7 minutes. I ordered them to be stationed at Paidhuni, Koka Bazaar, Nawab's Masjid, the junction of Erskine and Sandhurst roads, the J. J. Hospital corner, the Nall Bazaar and Doctor Street.

Having telephoned for the troops, I ordered the police to charge and disperse the mob. This they did with very good will and considerable success, though it was very difficult in the darkness to see what damage was done. Anyhow the mob dashed up the darker lanes and streets leading off Bhendy Bazaar and Paidhuni, and before they could collect again in force the troops had arrived. The sight of these put a check upon the mob's intentions and they gradually melted away for the time being.

Meanwhile, fearing that Kolsa Mohol1a, Chuna Batti and Halai Mohol1a would be subjected to a similar attack, I sent police to call them back at once to their Mohollas from the C division. The police discovered Kolsa Mohol1a and Halai Mohol1a and turned them back, but Chuna Batti had gone far ahead and was lost for the time being in the north of the C division. By the time, however, that it reached the Bhendy Bazaar I had posted the troops and the procession had therefore a comparatively quiet passage back to its Mohol1a.

I append a copy of Mr. Vincent's report to me on the disturbance in the early hours of Thursday morning.

13. In view of the rather serious situation created by the above circumstances I decided to leave the city for rest for 3 hours only. Mr. Vincent and I left at 6 a. m. and returned at 9 a. m., while Mr. Gadney stayed on till 9 a. m. and then went off on relief till 12 noon (on Thursday the 12th January). I also warned Rangari Mohol1a, Kolsa Mohol1a, Chuna Batti and Halai Mohol1a that if they wished to immerse their tabuts in the afternoon at Carnac Bandar, they must go straight down from their Mohollas to Carnac Road and not attempt to move up to and north of Paidhuni. They, however, refused to lift their tabuts or go out at all.

14. By 1 p. m. on Thursday it was fairly obvious that we were in for trouble. Huge crowds paraded the streets, and about 2 p. m. I received news that there was a certain amount of spasmodic stone-throwing at

Paidhuni. I had definite information that not a single Moholla would lift its tabut. Believing that there was likely to be trouble in the neighbourhood of Doctor Street, I remained on duty at Sulliman Chowkey, where I was joined by General Swann and Major Capper. About 4-40 p. m., as no further news had come from Paidhuni, I decided to go and lie down for a short time, as I had had only 4 hours' sleep on the morning of the 11th and none since. I went down Doctor Street to see that all was well and inspected the position there, and was making my way outside the Musalman quarter, when I was overtaken by the Commandant, Mounted Police, who told me that a message had just been received at Sulliman Chowkey to the effect that the situation at Paidhuni was very serious. I therefore rode straight back to Paidhuni.

On arrival there I found the road littered with new road-metal which was being flung at the police and the tram-cars and the military pickets by two large mobs situated, the one in Bhendy Bazaar and the other in Memonwada which debouches on Paidhuni. It was reported to me that about 4 p. m. the mob began to be very troublesome and the Paidhuni police went out with some mounted police to move them, but were forced to retire. At 4-15 the police again made a sally on the mob, but were stoned back again to Paidhuni. At about 4-30 p. m. the tram-traffic between the J. J. Hospital and Paidhuni came to a standstill. A European in a motor-car was stoned. The police then rushed out again and the mob retreated a little distance up Banian Row and Paidhuni Road and stoned them from there. Meanwhile a gang of Mahomedans at the junction of Chuna Batti was stoning carriages and trams. A tram-car in which a lady was seated was stopped by another gang and stones were thrown at the lady, who was hit on the left cheek. Then a number of Musalman youths got hold of the lady's skirts, and as far as Sub-Inspector Butterfield (who was coming up to her rescue) could see, tried to pull the lady out of the car. Sub-Inspector Butterfield and 3 privates of the Warwicks with 6 constables then appeared on the spot. They were met by a shower of road-metal, but forced the mob some 20 or 25 paces up Chuna Batti, whence they were continuously stoned. Each time that they retired the crowd pressed forward again. At about 5 p. m. their retreat was cut off by another mob, which commenced throwing stones from the opposite side in Banian Cross Road and Pinjrapur Road. At 5-10 Sub-Inspector Butterfield saw the military officer at Paidhuni signal to him and the soldiers to get away from the danger zone, and as their retreat was cut off and they were unable to fight their way through, they ensconced themselves behind a municipal urinal at the junction of Chuna Batti and held the crowd off until firing commenced. While in this position they were continuously stoned both from the street and from the houses. Among those injured by the stoning of the trams was a Hindu solicitor, whose companion reports that there was a group of Pathans with stones at Nawab's Masjid, and that the car in which he and his friend were sitting was stoned by bodies of rioters on both sides of Bhendy Bazaar from Nawab's Masjid to Paidhuni. Mr. Paton of Messrs. W. and A. Graham and Company, who had come down with his wife to see the tabut procession and occupied an upper room in a house at the corner of Memonwada and Bhendy Bazaar, reports that he had to close the windows of the room in the side and rear against stones that were flung from the street. In referring to a group of Pathans who halted under the verandah of the house he writes :—

> "In my twenty years' experience of this country I never before witnessed behaviour which so impressed me with a sense of sinister intentions."

Such was the position when I arrived about 5 p. m. The first thing I did was to ride forward a little way and have a look at both crowds. This produced a volley of road-metal. In the Memonwada crowd I observed 3 Pathans throwing stones and urging on the rest, and that established my conviction that the Pathans were on the war-path. My experience of previous disturbances shows that the Pathans at the very first sign of trouble begin to collect in small gangs at various points, and if the crowd once gets out of hand, they turn out in force and begin setting fire to shops and looting. This is unquestionably what they were preparing to do when I saw them.

I then looked at the Bhendy Bazaar mob, which completely covered the street as far as the eye could reach. In the front of it I noticed several boys throwing stones. I had already made up my mind that firing would have to be resorted to, as we had exhausted all attempts at pacific methods by Thursday morning at 3 a. m., and as also there was every possibility of the mob rising at Nall Bazaar, Two Tanks and Sulliman Chowkey, if the Bhendy Bazaar mob was not given a proper lesson. But I wanted to get rid of the boys first. Therefore about 5-10 p. m. I called the officer (Lieutenant Davies) in charge of the military picket and asked him to line up his men across both roads and place them in position to fire, but *not* to fire until they received the order to do so. I hoped that the appearance of the soldiers would (*a*) frighten the boys in the Bhendy Bazaar mob away and (*b*) induce the mob to cease throwing stones and disperse. As regards (*a*) the movement had the desired effect and the small boys bolted ; as regards (*b*) the mob retreated for a minute and then came forward again within 30 or 40 yards' distance of the soldiers and recommenced stoning them. I was standing immediately behind the soldiers and saw them dodging the metal, while a stone hit Lieutenant Davies, near whom I was standing. At about 5-17 p. m. Rao Bahadur Setalvad, 4th Presidency Magistrate, for whom I had telephoned at 5-10 p. m., arrived on the scene and I pointed out the general position to him and told him that I thought we should have to fire. He saw both mobs, he saw the troops being stoned, and he saw the condition of the road. At roughly 5-20 p. m. he gave the order to fire.

The troops fired 72 rounds and put an end to the disturbance. As a result of the firing, 14 persons were killed, 6 persons were injured and subsequently died in the hospital, and 27 were injured, of whom 6 were treated and discharged immediately. Of the dead, 7 were Hindus who were mixed up in the mob and the rest were Mahomedans ; and of the 27 injured, 19 were Mahomedans, 7 were Hindus and one was a Christian.

15. I greatly regret that we had to resort to extreme measures : but considering that the mob had been out at 3 a.m. and had had to be repulsed by the police, that the temper of the *badmash* element had been getting steadily worse, and that the mob collected again in the afternoon in spite of the presence of the troops; considering also that stone-throwing had been going on for fully an hour before I arrived at Paidhuni, that all traffic was stopped, that the police at Paidhuni had three times tried to clear the mob, that the Pathans were bent on mischief, and that I was very apprehensive of trouble in other parts of the

city if the disorder at Bhendy Bazaar was not put down very sharply, I am of opinion that by resorting to firing on the two mobs at Paidhuni we probably saved firing in other parts of the Musalman quarter and therefore greater loss of life. Government are aware how rapidly the spirit of tumult spreads, particularly among a populace like that of the Moharram celebrants, who belong to the lowest classes and actually regard the Mohorram, not as an opportunity for religious emotion but as the one chance vouchsafed them during the year of letting loose the forces of rascality and disorder and attacking the police and the public in more or less organised gangs. The information which I received from the *Katal-ki-rat* onwards showed that there was a definite intention to create disorder, and the fact that new road-metal had been collected in the lanes leading off Bhendy Bazaar clearly shows that an outbreak was contemplated. I believe firmly that, had we not taken extreme measures at Paidhuni, we should have had to face rioting throughout the whole area bounded by Two Tanks, Falkland Road and Bhendy Bazaar.

16. I also regret greatly the presence of Hindus amongst the killed and wounded. It is impossible on such occasions to protect the innocent; but considering that the crowd had collected and been throwing stones for fully an hour before firing took place and that the divisional police had warned them to disperse, it is a matter of great regret that the Hindus, if they were innocent, did not disappear. I do not think the firing of the troops was in any way haphazard or open to censure, for had it been so, they must have killed an old beggar woman who was sitting on the pavement of Bhendy Bazaar with rioters on both sides of her. On either side of her a man was shot, but she was left untouched, and was subsequently led into Paidhuni by the police.

On the other hand it is an undeniable fact that Hindus, and particularly the sectional bad characters amongst them, take a prominent part in the Moharram *tolis* and mob. Mr. Paton, who was an eye-witness of the whole outbreak, writes :—

"Under our eyes, and we were between the mob and troops all the while, the troops and police were murderously stoned, happily without any serious mishap, for close upon three-quarters of an hour. No law-abiding citizen had therefore any right to have been in either of the mobs and most certainly not at the late moment when the firing took place. If any were there at the outset of the stone-throwing he had most ample time and warning in which to get away, and if any stayed out of curiosity he had only himself to blame if he suffered along with the *badmashes* with whom he chose to herd."

17. Just after the firing ceased and both mobs had disappeared, General Swann arrived at Paidhuni; and at his suggestion I called up from the Head Police Office the balance of the Warwickshire Regiment, and from Marine Lines 4 companies of the 96th Berár Infantry. These were posted at once throughout the disturbed area. The measures taken at Paidhuni, however, had such an effect that by 10 p. m. I was able to draw off some of the military from each picket. By 12 midnight on Thursday I was able to send all British troops back to barracks, and by 12 midnight on Sunday the 15th January I was able to send back all the native infantry and reduce the police guard. This was partly due to the action of the police on Friday and Saturday in arresting a large number of persons who were identified as having played a prominent part in the disturbances of Thursday morning and Thursday afternoon. All those persons against whom definite evidence is forthcoming are being placed before the magistracy. By Friday morning all was outwardly quiet and the City had resumed its normal aspect. Since then there has been nothing to record beyond the fact that the bad characters of a particular type, who signalize their mode of life by wearing their hair long in front and curled, have had their locks cropped by the barber for fear of being arrested by the police as participants in the *toli* disturbances.

18. There are certain points in this sorry business of the Moharram of 1911, which give some cause for satisfaction :—

First.—The police carried out their orders regarding Doctor Street to the very letter and kept it hermetically closed from the first to the last day.

Secondly.—The self-restraint shewn by Mr. Vincent, the European officers, the 4 sowars and the native foot police, who accompanied the Rangari Moholla tabut from the J. J. Hospital to Paidhuni in the early hours of the 12th under a continuous attack with stones, lighted wood and *làthis,* is worthy of commendation.

Thirdly.—The material support which was received from General Swann and his staff went far towards recompensing the Police Commissioner for the anxiety of a ten days' struggle to checkmate the forces of disorder. General Swann himself spent the 6th night with me at Sulliman Chowkey up to 4 a. m., with the sole object of shewing the public that he and I were working together. And many must have recognized him and drawn their own conclusions. General Swann was also present at Sulliman Chowkey on the last day and also at Paidhuni. I cannot sufficiently express my thanks for his help, and for the ready assistance afforded by Lieut-Colonel H. R. Vaughan and his regiment, and subsequently by Colonel Powys Lane and the 96th Berár Infantry.

Fourthly.—I must express my thanks to Inspector Khan Bahadur Shaikh Ibrahim and the Mahomedan officers of the Criminal Investigation Department for their continuous efforts throughout a period of nearly three weeks to smooth away all difficulties and keep the Mohollas in a good temper. That their efforts ultimately proved fruitless was no fault of theirs, but was due to circumstances beyond their control. I have a lively sense of their unremitting efforts to ensure a peaceful Moharram.

Fifthly.—Mr. Ardeshir Umrigar deserves special mention in that for a period of a week he supplied free of all cost at Paidhuni, Sulliman Chowkey and Nall Bazaar mineral waters, tea, coffee, sandwiches and light refreshments for the use of the European police officers who were on continuous duty at and near those points both by day and night. For the native constables who were in the streets for ten days and nights and who had no time to go to their homes, I provided 2 annas *per diem* apiece to enable them to buy a meal and tea. A portion, if not the whole of the sum thus involved, has been offered to me by Rao Bahadur Keshavji N. Sailor, so that possibly I may not have to ask Government to sanction this extra but necessary expenditure.

Sixthly.—Credit is due to Badlu and the Madanpura Julhais for accepting the position, keeping their promise to me, and performing their Moharram and tabut immersion in the regular way without giving the smallest trouble to the police.

Seventhly.—Great credit is due to the divisional police of all ranks for the manner in which they performed a vigil of ten days and nights and for the self-restraint which they shewed in dealing with the mob.

19. In conclusion, I must raise the question as to what should be our policy for the future in regard to the Moharram. As matters are at present, there is no vestige of religion or religious fervour in the *toli*-processions and the tabut-processions. On the contrary the Moharram has become, and is utilized as merely an excuse for rascality to burst its usual barriers and flow over the city in a current of excessive turbulence. For ten days every year the Hindu merchants are blackmailed and harassed until they pay a contribution to the cost of the processions; the police, who are not half numerous enough to guard the whole area involved, are kept in the streets for ten days and nights and ordinary police work simply disappears, as there is no officer at the police-stations to record complaints and no native police to take up an enquiry; a large portion of the Shia population has to evacuate its houses and take refuge in Sálsette for fear of insult and assault; and in the end, if the police hold fast and insist upon rascality keeping within certain limits, the city has to face the distressing spectacle of open disorder and its complement of drastic repression.

The only unobjectionable features of the ten days' celebration are the nightly *Waaz* or religious discourses by chosen preachers. But, unfortunately, these are little patronized by those to whom they would do most good, namely, the bad characters in the *tolis*.

Statement made by Mr. N. J. Paton, J. P., partner in the firm of Messrs. W. & A. Graham & Co.

On Thursday, 12th January, at 2 p. m., at the invitation of a Mahomedan friend I went with Mrs. Paton to the house at the junction of Parel Road and Kolsa Moholla (otherwise Memonwada) with a view to witnessing the Moharram procession.

The house, on the first floor where we were, has windows at the back and on the Kolsa Moholla side and a verandah on the Parel Road side, the latter affording a clear view down the Parel Road and of the open space in front of the Paidhuni Police Station.

The crowd came and went without much incident until about 3, when two Mahomedans were brought up under arrest amid a good deal of apparently sympathetic shouting on the part of the on-lookers.

After that the temper of the crowd seemed to change; but, although several carriages with European ladies drove past, they were suffered to do so without molestation.

I was not myself then anxious, but my Mahomedan friend at about 4 o'clock warned me that the crowd was now anything but peaceably disposed. Shortly thereafter I became apprehensive of coming trouble on noting the overt truculent bearing of the Pathans, of whom there were many, and notably of a group which halted for some time under our verandah. In my twenty years' experience of the country I never before witnessed behaviour which so impressed me with a sense of sinister intentions.

At about 4-30 the police made a systematic attempt to clear the pavements and street in front of the Police Station down to opposite our verandah.

This the crowd resented and there was considerable hooting.

A few minutes later one stone was thrown from the crowd in Kolsa Moholla, and almost immediately stone-throwing of a very serious and dangerous kind commenced on both sides of us.

We were obliged to close our windows at the back and Kolsa Moholla side; but, although numerous stones fell on our house, none entered and no one was injured.

From the verandah it was possible to see not only what was going on in Parel Road but also to note the fusillade of stones that came from Kolsa Moholla.

The trams were still running in Parel Road; and, as each passed the end of Goghari Moholla, it was met by murderous volleys of stones, which by pure luck alone failed to result in most serious consequences to the passengers.

Occasionally the police endeavoured to keep the crowd at a distance by themselves throwing stones.

In this way half an hour passed, when about 5 o'clock or thereabouts Mr. Edwardes arrived and took charge.

Under his direction the detachment of the Warwicks, which had been standing under arms in the neighbourhood all the afternoon, was drawn in line across Parel Road and Kolsa Moholla and knelt down in readiness to fire.

The officer in charge waved his handkerchief in the hope that any law-abiding persons who might still be in the crowd would clear away.

About 5-15 Mr. Setalwad and Mr. Vincent arrived; and, as the stone-throwing was then proceeding as vigorously as ever, Mr. Setalwad gave the order to fire, an order that was immediately carried out. After two or three volleys, occupying about a minute, "cease firing" was ordered.

The mob had by this time cleared off, leaving between thirty and forty dead and wounded.

It is said some innocent Hindus have suffered. I hardly think this is possible.

If the troops had fired hurriedly it might have been so, but they did not fire without the most ample warning.

Under our eyes, and we were between the mob and the troops all the while, the troops and Police were murderously stoned, happily without any serious mishap, for close upon three-quarters of an hour.

No law-abiding citizen had, therefore, any right to have been in either of the mobs and most certainly not at the late moment when the firing took place. If any were there at the outset of the stone-throwing he had most ample time and warning in which to get away, and if any stayed out of curiosity he had only himself to blame if he suffered along with the *badmashes* with whom he chose to herd.

It is impossible to under-estimate the seriousness of what might have occurred if the drastic lesson that was administered had been longer delayed, and it is puerile for those who were not present to presume to criticise it.

The two mobs numbered many thousands of the most lawless and fanatical men in the city, and the manner in which the fusillade of stones was started and kept up indicates clearly that stones must have been purposely brought to the ground in readiness for the fight and in very considerable quantity.

Viewing the situation as a whole, I consider that the mob without doubt was given more leniency than it had any right to expect, and that to have postponed the firing any longer, or to have restricted the firing to a single volley, must inevitably have seriously imperilled the safety of a large section of the city and would have involved much greater bloodshed than unhappily occurred, before order could have been restored.

Those who were eye-witnesses like myself can hold but one opinion as to the judgment, restraint and patience with which, in circumstances of intolerable and protracted provocation, Mr. Edwardes dealt with a situation of extreme gravity and difficulty.

RESOLUTION.—The Governor-in-Council has given careful consideration to the reports of the disturbance which took place in the city of Bombay on 12th January, 1911 on the occasion of the Moharram festival. He is of opinion that the police acted throughout with great discretion and restraint and that the final appeal to military force was necessary for the public security. The loss of life which occurred is much to be regretted, but the military do not appear to have done more than was consistent with dispersing the mob. The Governor-in-Council desires to express his thanks to the military authorities for the prompt assistance rendered by them and to Mr. Edwardes, Commissioner of Police, and the force under his charge, for their great exertions throughout the whole period of the Moharram.

2. It now remains to consider the measures to be taken for the future. Government have done all that lay within their power to enable the Moharram processions to be held with due regard to the safety of the law-abiding mass of the community, but without success. In 1909 and 1910 there were no processions; but this year, as in 1908, in spite of every precaution there were scenes of disorder and violence which had ultimately to be quelled by military force with considerable loss of life. Government cannot allow the recurrence of such disturbances, and it has become necessary to consider whether the procession of tabuts, with their attendant *tolis,* should not be prohibited next year. Before arriving at any final decision, however, Government trust that the Mahomedan community will, through their leaders or otherwise, endeavour to concert effective measures to secure that, while the religious character of the observance of the Moharram is retained, there may be a reasonable guarantee that it shall not again degenerate into lawlessness, discreditable to all concerned and gravely injurious to the interests of Bombay. The Governor-in-Council will be ready to give the most careful consideration to any such proposals, but it will be possible to adopt them only if they seem to provide a reasonable guarantee against any future disturbance of the peace.

3. In this connection the leaders of the Mahomedan community could do much to assist the cause of law and order by explaining to the people that the tabut processions and *tolis* are in no way necessary to the religious celebration of the Moharram. Government have received information that for many years Kâzis in Sind have been issuing *fatwâs* inveighing against the degradation of the mourning ceremony into processions of jesters and mountebanks, and that in the town of Sujāwal the people have themselves put a stop to all tabut processions.

By order of His Excellency the Honourable the Governor-in-Council,

C. A. KINCAID,
Secretary to Government.

INDEX

D

E

F

G

H

I

J

K

L

M

W